East-West in Art

Patterns of Aesthetic and Cultural Relationships

Buckle: A "Scythian" Alexander

Bactrian, 2nd century B. C. or later (bronze, w., 3 in.)
Heeramaneck Collection, New York

This is a perfect example of fusion between a Western subject and an Eastern motif. The rider is clearly inspired by the figure on horseback from the Alexander Sarcophagus (now in Istanbul), while the theme of the hunt of wild animals is a standard one for such so-called Scythian ornaments.

EAST-WEST IN ART

Patterns of Cultural &
Aesthetic Relationships

by THEODORE BOWIE *in collaboration with* J. LEROY DAVIDSON
JANE GASTON MAHLER
RICHARD B. REED
WILLIAM SAMOLIN
DOROTHY G. SHEPHERD
DENIS SINOR
with an introduction by RUDOLF WITTKOWER

INDIANA UNIVERSITY PRESS/ BLOOMINGTON & LONDON

Copyright © 1966 by Indiana University Press
Library of Congress Catalog Card Number: 66-12723
Manufactured in the United States of America
SECOND PRINTING 1967

NOTES ON THE AUTHORS

THEODORE BOWIE is a member of the Department of Fine Arts at Indiana University, in charge of courses in Oriental art. He was the organizer and director of the internationally circulated exhibition of the Arts of Thailand, and editor of the catalog which accompanied it. He is also the author, among other works, of *The Drawings of Hokusai* and *An American Orientalist: Langdon Warner Through His Letters*.

J. LEROY DAVIDSON teaches Oriental art at the University of California at Los Angeles, with India and China as his particular fields. He is the author of *The Lotus Sutra in Chinese Art*.

JANE GASTON MAHLER is a member of the Department of Art History and Archaeology at Columbia University, specializing in Oriental art. She is the author of *The Westerners Among the Figurines of the T'ang Dynasty*.

RICHARD B. REED is Curator of the Bernardo Mendel Collection in the Lilly Rare Book Library at Indiana University.

WILLIAM SAMOLIN, a member of the Department of Art History and Archaeology at Columbia University, specializes in technical analysis of archaeological finds in Asia and has written numerous scientific papers on the subject.

DOROTHY G. SHEPHERD is Curator of the Department of Textiles and Near Eastern Art at the Cleveland Museum of Art; she is the author of authoritative studies in those fields.

DENIS SINOR is the Chairman of the Department of Uralic and Altaic Studies at Indiana University. A historian specializing in Central Asia, he is the author of *Introduction à l'Etude de l'Eurasie Centrale* and a *History of Hungary*.

RUDOLF WITTKOWER is Chairman of the Department of Art History and Archaeology at Columbia University. Primarily an authority on Renaissance architecture, he has a wide range of scholarly interests. He is the author of *Art and Architecture in Italy, 1600 to 1750* and *Italian Architecture in the Age of Humanism* and, in collaboration with his wife, *Born Under Saturn*.

Design by   David Ahlsted
Melvin M. Miller
George Sadek

CONTENTS

Indiana University International Studies

Publication of this book has been assisted by the
International Affairs Center of Indiana University

EAST AND WEST, ORIENT AND OCCIDENT, HAVE IN THE COURSE OF THE CENTURIES DESCRIBED MANY WIDELY DIVERGENT AREAS IN THAT IMMENSE STRETCH WHICH LIES BETWEEN KAMCHATKA and the Gates of Hercules. The lands to which one or another of those appellations has been applied expand and contract, and there is no permanent boundary line separating some theoretical East from an imaginary West. Everything is relative here, and we must set our marks carefully in time and space. For the purposes of this book, East refers to the lands east of the Urals—what we usually mean by Asia—and West includes Europe with its extensions into the Americas. Africa and the South Seas are arbitrarily omitted. Our span of time starts about the first millennium B. C., in the Bronze Age, and reaches into the present.

Within this vast territorial unit a ceaseless and varied series of movements, from one end to the other, from both ends to the middle, and from the center outward in both directions, have been taking place for the last 3000 years. In the earliest epochs this flux was impeded presumably only by geographical obstacles; later, political and religious boundaries were created as well. Various peoples, sometimes nomads in search of water or grass, tradesmen, often missionaries and pilgrims, and periodically, conquering invaders or explorers, have been constantly on the march within the Eurasian continent. What they found when they settled, what they brought with them, what they took back if they ever went back, are not abstract concepts but concrete artifacts that can be collected, analyzed, and displayed. These may be armor and trappings, coins, images and symbols—basically, forms that have substance and color. They constitute a kind of universal artistic currency, one form being affected by another by the very fact of the exchange. We can study such objects for examples of influences and counter-influences, of cultural borrowings and cross-fertilizations; parallels, affinities and coincidences, identities, contrasts and differences appear, and we may seek to interpret all of this by probing the motivations and analyzing the circumstances which governed the making of these objects.

This broad and endlessly complicated subject can be treated here only through a very general examination of some of its easily grasped phases. The originality of this study lies in its combination of the descriptive approach, which rests on historical sequence, with the technique of confrontation, which is essentially a matter of aesthetic comparisons. The initial inspiration for this work grew out of an exhibition organized at Indiana University for the Fourth Quadrennial Conference on East-West Cultural and Literary Relationships, during the summer of 1966. The end result is a text illustrated by more than 300 plates, which extends the original exhibition; in fact the work has become an exhibition between book covers.

The question of East-West artistic relationships has occupied the attention of scholars for a long time, and the general public has been afforded tantalizing glimpses of it in several large exhibitions, of which the most notable (but by no means the only ones) have been *Art in Asia and the West*, prepared in 1957 by Dr. Grace McCann Morley for the San Francisco Museum of Art; the slightly earlier pair, *East-West* and *West-East,* which the Royal Ontario Museum of Toronto put on in 1952-53; the great *Orient-Occident* exhibition organized on behalf of UNESCO in Paris in 1958-59 and displayed at the Musée Cernuschi; and *East & West,* a bibliographical exhibition arranged by Princeton University in 1957. Our indebtedness to such illustrious predecessors is hereby duly recognized. The numerous smaller and more specialized shows, and a number of books dealing with various elements of the problem, are referred to in relevant discussions throughout this book.

East-West in Art is a collaborative effort: though the point of view of the art historian may seem to prevail, we also hear from the general historian, the museum specialist, the bibliographer, and the analytical archaeologist. Would that we could have added the mythologist, the folklore specialist, the anthropologist, and the experts on such trans-national phenomena as Islam and the Pan-Slavic movement, among others. There is no end to the ramifications of our subject, and we can only hope that others will continue and perfect what we have essayed here. My first thanks as Editor are therefore due to the authors of the separate chapters, not only for their written contributions, but for their aid in suggesting illustrations and helping to obtain photographs, and, in some cases, negotiating loans. (Because they were out of the country when this book was being printed, Professors Davidson and Mahler did not have the opportunity of checking the final proofs of their chapters.)

I am obligated to so many people across the land for ideas, suggestions, loans of objects, and help of all kinds that it seems best to group them geographically: in Washington, D.C., Mr. Alan Fern of the Prints and Photographs Division of the Library of Congress, and at the Freer Gallery Mr. James Cahill (now at the University of California at Berkeley); at Princeton University, Professor Wen Fong and Mr. Roderick Whitfield, both of the Department of Art and Archaeology; at Columbia University, Professor Rudolf Wittkower, who, in addition to furnishing valuable advice, agreed to write the Introduction to this volume, and Professors Meyer Schapiro and Samuel Eilenberg; at the Metropolitan Museum of Art, Mr. Aschwin Lippe, Mr. A. Hyatt Mayor, Dr. Ernst Grube, and Miss Jean Schmitt, all members of the curatorial staff; at the Cooper Union Museum for the Arts of Decoration, Mr. Edward Kallop and Miss Alice B. Beer; at the Brooklyn Museum, Dr. B. von Bothmer; at the New York Public Library, Dr. Karl Kup; at the Pierpont Morgan Library, Mr. Frederick B. Adams, Jr., and Dr. John M. Plummer; and Mr. Gordon Washburn, Director of the Asia House Gallery; among the collectors in New York City, Mr. John M. Crawford, Jr., Mr. Norbert Schimmel, Dr. Arthur Sackler, and Professor Ulfert Wilke; among the New York dealers in Oriental art, Mr. Ralph M. Chait, Mr. Frank Caro, Mr. Nasli Heeramaneck, the Mahboubian Gallery, and Miss Marian Willard; in New Haven, Mr. George J. Lee of the Yale University Art Gallery; in Boston, the late Robert Treat Paine, who, until his untimely death, was Curator of Asiatic Art in the Museum of Fine Arts; in Cambridge, Professors Benjamin Rowland and Usher Coolidge, and Mr. Carey Welch of the Fogg Museum, and Mr.

Philip Hofer of the Houghton Library; in Toronto, Mr. Henry Trubner, Curator of Oriental Art in the Royal Ontario Museum; in Cleveland, Mr. Sherman E. Lee, Director of the Cleveland Museum of Art; at the Art Institute of Chicago, Miss Margaret Gentles, Mr. Jack Sewell, and Mr. Harold Joachim, all of the curatorial staff; in Kansas City, Missouri, Mr. Laurence Sickman, Director of the William Rockhill Nelson Gallery of Art; in Seattle, Dr. Richard Fuller, Director of the Seattle Art Museum; and at the University of Michigan in Ann Arbor, Professors Charles Sawyer and Oleg Grabar.

Among my associates at Indiana University, I must cite Professors Henry Hope, Henry Smith, and Albert Elsen, and Mrs. Peggy Gilfoy, Registrar of the University Art Museum; Mr. David Randall, Librarian of the Lilly Rare Book Library, a direct participant in our enterprise; Professor Horst Frenz, permanent chairman of the Quadrennial East-West Conferences. At the Indiana University Press, Miss Edith R. Greenburg and Mrs. Lou Ann Brower have labored long and effectively in the preparation and revision of a very complex text. My colleague, George Sadek, is responsible for the splendid design of the book. The generous grants-in-aid made by the Research Committee of the Graduate School, under former Dean John W. Ashton, and the Committee for International Studies, under Professor Robert Byrnes, are also gratefully acknowledged. I am also indebted to Miss Carol Peden of the Press for her help.

Thanks are also due for the courtesy of various museums in making available and permitting the reproduction of photographs of works in their possession: the National Gallery, the Textile Museum, and the Library of Congress, in Washington, D. C.; the Walters Gallery in Baltimore; the Metropolitan Museum, the Museum of Modern Art, the Cooper Union Museum, and the Brooklyn Museum in New York; the Boston Museum of Fine Arts; the Royal Ontario Museum; the Cleveland Museum of Art; the Detroit Institute of Fine Arts; the John Herron Museum of Indianapolis; the Art Institute of Chicago; the Minneapolis Institute of Art; the William Rockhill Nelson Gallery of Art, Kansas City, Missouri; the Seattle Art Museum; the Cincinnati Art Museum; and the Wadsworth Atheneum in Hartford, Connecticut.

January, 1966
Bloomington

THEODORE BOWIE

WESTERN EUROPE	ROME	GREECE	EGYPT	ASIA MINOR	MESOPOTAMIA	IRAN
		Minoan Art	Empire			
		Dorian		Hittites		
		Invasion		(1475-1192)		
1000 Bronze Age					Assyria	
	Etruscans	*Iliad &*			(884-626)	Luristan
		Odyssey				Bronzes
						Achaemenian
		Parthenon	Alexander's Conquests			Empire (550-330)
			(336-323)			
0	——— Empire ———					
	Trade with		Crucifixion			
100	China					
200						
300						Sasanian Empire
						(226-661)
400 Barbaric Invasions						
500						
		↑		Hagia Sophia		
600				(532)		
					Birth of Islam	
700					(ca. 625)	
800 Charlemagne						
900						
1000						
						Seljuk Dynasty
1100 Romanesque Art		Byzantine Empire				(1037-1258)
1200 Gothic Art						
Marco Polo's Travels						Mongol Dynasty
1300 (1271-1292)				Ottoman Empire		(1258-1337)
1400						Timurid Dynasty
Renaissance Art		↓ Fall of Constantinople				(1387-1449)
1500 Columbus' Voyages		(1453)				
						Safavid Dynasty
1600 Vasco da Gama's Voyages						(1499-1736)
1700 Baroque Art						
Chinoiserie	Discovery of Pompeii					
1800 Romantic Art						
Orientalism						
1900						

INDIA	S. E. ASIA	CENTRAL ASIA	SIBERIA	CHINA	JAPAN	
Aryan Invasion		Bronze Age		Bronze Age		
				Shang Dynasty (1523-1028)		
Vedic Hymns		Minussinsk Mounds				1000
			Ordos Mounds			
				Chou Dynasties (1028-281)		
Buddha (563-483)					Jomon	
Maurya Empire (322-185)				Han Dynasties (206 B.C.-221 A.D.)	Bronze Age	0
					Yayoi	100
					Haniwa	200
Bactria & Parthia		Buddhist Shrines		Six Dynasties (220-577)		300
Gandhara						400
Gupta Empire (320-647)						500
						600
				T'ang Dynasty (618-906)	Introduction of Buddhism	
Medieval Dynasties						700
	Borobudur					800
						900
Moslem Invasions				Sung Dynasty		1000
Chola Empire (850-1100)	Angkor Wat			(960-1279)		1100
			Genghiz Khan's Conquests (1180-1227)			1200
				Yüan Dynasty		1300
				(1260-1368)		
				Ming Dynasty		1400
		Tamerlane's Conquests (1358-1405)		(1368-1644)		
Mughal Dynasty (1526-1761)						1500
					Momoyama	1600
				Ch'ing Dynasty (1644-1912)	(1574-1603) Tokugawa	1700
British Raj (1761-1948)					(1603-1868) Portuguese & Dutch Trade	1800
					Perry Expedition	1900
Partition & Republic				Republic		

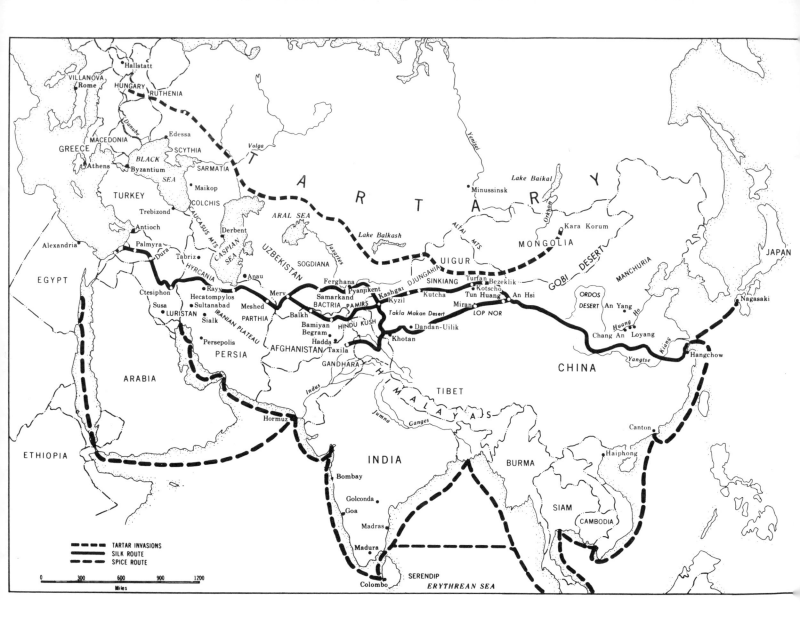

Villanova
Rome
Hallstatt
HUNGARY RUTHENIA
Danube
MACEDONIA
GREECE
SCYTHIA
Edessa
BLACK
Athens
Byzantium
SEA
Maikop
TURKEY
SARMATIA
COLCHIS
Trebizond
CAUCASUS MTS.
Antioch
Derbent
Alexandria
Palmyra
Dura
Tabriz
HYRCANIA
EGYPT
Ctesiphon
Rayy
Susa
Hecatompylos
LURISTAN
Sultanabad
Sialk
Persepolis
PERSIA
ARABIA

ARAL SEA
Lake Balkash
UZBEKISTAN
SOGDIANA
Jaxartes
CASPIAN SEA
Anau
Volga
Ferghana
Merv
Pyanjikent
Meshed
Samarkand
PARTHIA
Balkh
BACTRIA
PAMIRS
Bamiyan
Begram
HINDU KUSH
IRANIAN PLATEAU
AFGHANISTAN
Hadda
Taxila
GANDHARA
HIMALAYAS
Indus
Jumna
Ganges

TARTARY
Yenisei
Minussinsk
Lake Baikal
Orkhon
ALTAI MTS.
Kara Korum
MONGOLIA
UIGUR
GOBI DESERT
DJUNGARIA
SINKIANG
Turfan
Bezeklik
Kashgar
Kotscho
Kutcha
An Hsi
Kyzil
Tun Huang
ORDOS DESERT
An Yang
Takla Makan Desert
Miran
LOP NOR
Huang
Ho
Khotan
Dandan-Uilik
Chang An
Loyang
CHINA
Kiang
Yangtse
TIBET
Hormuz

JAPAN
MANCHURIA
Nagasaki
Hangchow
Canton
Haiphong
BURMA
SIAM
CAMBODIA

Bombay
Golconda
Goa
Madras
INDIA
Madura
SERENDIP
Colombo
ERYTHREAN SEA

- - - TARTAR INVASIONS
——— SILK ROUTE
— — SPICE ROUTE

0   300   600   900   1200
Miles

ETHIOPIA

IN THE LAST TWO OR THREE GENERATIONS AN EVER-GROWING
NUMBER OF SCHOLARS HAVE TURNED THEIR ATTENTION TO THE
LINKS BETWEEN THE ARTS OF EUROPE AND OF NON-EUROPEAN
civilizations, but this vast problem has never been approached and
investigated in its entirety. Nor has such an attempt been made in
the present book. But the project that has here come to life is extremely ambitious—more ambitious, more varied and extensive in
approach, viewpoints, and historical perspectives than any other work
dealing with East-West relations. In this Introduction I propose to submit some points of a general nature, points that may help to gauge
the character and complexity of the present enterprise. We are concerned with cultural and artistic exchanges over immensely wide
spaces—6000, 7000 miles, and more. While this does not present
a problem in the age of jet propulsion, the question must be asked,
and has often been asked, how such distances were traversed in times
long past when the means of locomotion were primitive.

For almost a century ethnologists have worked with two antago-
nistic theories: diffusion of techniques, ideas, concepts, and art forms
versus independent, "spontaneous generation" of culture in different
parts of the world. These mutually exclusive working methods have
been hotly debated ever since A. Bastian, in the second half of the
nineteenth century, propounded his evolutionary thesis that similar
cultural characteristics arise at parallel phases in the development of
different societies. The advocates of diffusionism and the defend-
ers of independent convergence are still at each others' throats.
Their discussions pertain mainly to pre-literary civilizations. For the
high civilizations with literary traditions diffusionism has been developed into a universally accepted technique of research; in art-
historical controversies the degree and character of diffusion may be
debated, but the principle of diffusion is not called into question.

The unqualified acceptance of diffusionism is a tacit premise of
most of the papers in this book. The historian of culture or art who,
through the study of high civilizations, has learned to operate with dif-
fusionist interchanges is more readily prepared than the ethnologist
to extend the method to nonliterary, so-called primitive cultures. Nobody can deny that the artifacts of the northern nomad tribes, discussed in Professor Samolin's paper, found distribution over an
enormous area, though the precise roads of transmission may never
be traceable.

Acceptance of diffusion does not, however, preclude the possibility
of convergence and parallelism of cultural phenomena. In the first
chapter an attempt is made to explain similar developments in art
styles East and West in terms of reaction to, and sublimation of, the
prevailing cultural ambience. Though such explanations cannot claim
to do more than provide suggestive analogies between cultural and
artistic manifestations, the fact remains that certain art forms, which
we conventionally designate as archaic, classic, baroque, etc., recur
in widely separate civilizations at unrelated periods, a sign perhaps of
the comparative dearth of basic artistic expressions, the world over,
at the disposal of our species.

The ultimate test of diffusion lies, of course, in the proof of the existence of definitely traceable roads of migration. Even in prehistoric times there existed caravan roads bridging the vast expanses of the Asian land-mass between China and Europe, a northern route via the Caspian and Black Seas and a southern route via the highland of Iran and Syria. In historic times, the Romans, who kept the southern road open for hundreds of years, imported much coveted silk from China. Although the road was virtually cut with Arab ascendancy and was reopened only in the middle of the thirteenth century when the *pax mongolica* had pacified the largest part of Asia, the areas along this road always remained the great melting pot of cultural and artistic currents. Professor Mahler's chapter contains a sketch of the events along the eastern stretches of the "silk route" for over a thousand years, and Miss Shepherd demonstrates the perennial part played by Iran as buffer, bridge, and focal point in the varying fortunes of East-West exchanges. But just when the material regarding the roads of transmission is ample, we must sharpen our critical judgment, for the pitfalls of superficial affinities may lead and have led to strange misconceptions.

A famous test case may illustrate the seriousness of the charge. During the hundred years of Mongol domination of Asia, East and West drew closer together than ever before. In 1245 Pope Innocent IV sent the Franciscan John of Plano di Carpini as envoy to the court of the Grand Khan; in 1253 William of Rubruck followed him as envoy of Louis IX of France. The brothers Nicolo and Maffeo Polo, who left Venice in 1255, traveled fourteen years through Asia. When they set out on a second journey in 1271, they were accompanied by their young son and nephew Marco, who remained in East Asia until 1295. While Marco Polo's account has no equal, there were many other travelers at this period who have left fascinating records of their experience, such men as John of Monte Corvino, the founder of the Latin Church in China, who remained there from about 1293 to his death in 1328; Andrew of Perugia, who was engaged in missionary work in Peking between about 1308 and 1318; Friar Odoric, who spent six years—between 1322 and 1328—in northern China; John of Marignolli who reached Peking at the head of a papal embassy in 1342; and Francesco Balducci Pegolotti, the agent of the Florentine house of Bardi who wrote, in about 1340, a kind of merchant's manual concerning the trade with the East. Some of these names appear in the contexts of chapters 6 and 7.

The long period of peace when, according to Pegolotti, the trade routes were secure, when Franciscan friars set up convents in China and Genoese merchants had a settlement at the port of Zaiton north of Canton, came to an end in 1368. In that year the Tatar dynasty was driven out by a revolution and was replaced by the native Ming dynasty. From then on and for the better part of 200 years an iron curtain shut off Europe from China.

The rich contacts between Europe and China that had flourished from the mid-thirteenth to the mid-fourteenth century have fired the imagination of some scholars. As is shown in chapter 6, they con-

Clarification of the roads of transmission is only the first step when dealing with the problem of diffusion. In considering the transplantation of forms, designs, and styles, we are faced with a triple challenge, from the simplest cases—the trading of objects and the migration of artisans—to the assimilation and adaptation of imported material, and then to its complete transformation. On the level of such artisan media as ceramics, metalwork, and textiles, modern techniques of research make it possible to establish conclusively how this kind of import was assimilated and transformed in a new cultural environment. Chapter 5 contains a number of excellent examples. But when we have to deal with works of "high art" such as painting and sculpture, the same questions are more difficult to answer, owing to the fact that such creations are inseparable from philosophical and religious concepts. Even where, in the process of translation from one civilization to another, essentials of stylistic formulas or representational patterns survive, their meaning may have changed beyond recognition. This kind of change is surely true for the formal typology of the ancient Near East that re-emerged, Christianized, in Romanesque art; for Greco-Roman sculpture that reached India, and even China, transformed through Buddhist Gandhara mediation; and for much of the orientalism and exoticism that invaded Europe in recent centuries.

It is rarely possible to recapture fully the thought processes behind the more complex transmissions and transformations. The fairly well-documented Sinomania in eighteenth-century Europe allows some insight into the nature of this kind of quest. Thinkers of the Enlightenment embraced wholeheartedly Confucius' moral philosophy which, based upon reason and tolerance, seemed to offer a better foundation for a harmonious communal life than a revealed religion with its fanaticism, obscurantism, and intolerance. One is inclined to conclude that some people endeavored to establish the physical conditions for the Chinese way of life by imitating Chinese art, architecture, and nature. When Father Matteo Ripa's views of the imperial gardens at Jehol reached London in 1724, they influenced the beginnings of the English landscape garden movement, because they were regarded as visual proofs of the informal approach to nature in a free society governed by wise, just, and temperate rulers. Thus it was the erroneous belief in a political utopia come true in China that stimulated borrowings in the artistic sphere. Admittedly, for a fuller discussion of Europe's enchantment with the arts of China, many other aspects would have to be considered.

There is a large body of cultural material, perhaps best subsumed under the vague terms "symbols" and "archetypal images," that we encounter through long periods of time and wide spaces, the origins of which are lost in the early dawn of history. The gammadion or swastika, the winged globe, the Tree of Life, the eagle and snake, the Great Mother, the mythical hero as animal-tamer, the dragon, and the totemistic fauna of animals and monsters all form part of this material. Scholars who tread this complex territory diverge widely, for the permutations of both type and meaning seem almost infinite. Nevertheless, such symbols no longer elude the persistent and judicious investigator who, by inquiring into their pedigree and history, can often throw unexpected light on the give-and-take between East and West. Only two symbols have here been analyzed (in chapters 8 and 9), but those for a good reason, for both the "Barbarian" and the "Universal Hero" are specific concepts of high civilizations and point to an East-West cultural homogeneity, at least in some respects.

To talk of cultural homogeneity of East and West may sound strange, but let us recall a few simple and obvious facts. Large mountain ranges bisect the Asian land-mass and its western peninsula, Europe, into a southern half with rich geological formations and continuous access to the open sea and a northern half with wide, inner-continental, almost featureless plains that stretch from the Pacific to the Atlantic. All the high civilizations of antiquity—China, India, Persia, Babylonia, Egypt, Greece, and Rome—lay in the southern belt. They all were urban civilizations with—broadly speaking—similarly structured societies. They all developed classic literatures, believed in a similar moral code and boasted great law-givers and founders of religions. They all produced monumental stone buildings and monumental sculpture and painting, focussed on the representation of godhead, man, and beast. But despite such homogeneity, variety is the hallmark of these civilizations. Each had developed a distinct character of its own that was maintained throughout history.

By contrast, the wide steppes of the northern belt produced a fairly uniform nomad or semi-nomad civilization without any of the features peculiar to the southern urban civilizations. Thus, nomad art is the very antithesis of southern monumental art: nomad art is confined to portable objects, to weapons, implements of daily use, and personal ornaments (see chapter 3); this art is, moreover, intrinsically abstract and, in spite of sober observation, tends to ornamentalize animal and man. The constant pressure of the semi-barbaric nations, from the northern borders of China all along the Asian mountain barrier to the Danube and the European heartland, erupted from time to time and engulfed the high civilizations. Obviously, the interpenetration of nomad and high-culture art continued without interruption for over two thousand years. But the symbol of the Barbarian could neither arise nor be assimilated among the nomads: they *were* the barbarians to the mind of all civilized peoples.

As is suggested in chapter 8, the stranger, the foreigner, the barbarian, and the race that is different were often endowed with grotesque and monstrous appearances. But misshapen men and animals, hybrid formations, hallucinatory deformations played a part in the thought and imagery of all peoples at all times. The tenacious belief in monsters—helpmates and evildoers, gods and demons—leads into the substratum of magic conceptions and rituals. "Man makes the demons in the image of his own savage and irrational passions" (Jane Harrison). The rise of Greek civilization is symbolized by the victory of the Olympian gods over chthonic monsters. Yet at the same time the Greeks created a large repository of monstrosities. Derived from the East, they were handed back to the East; they also nourished the

European conception of monsters down the ages. East and West thus responded to the same galaxy of monsters.

The problem of cultural homogeneity linking Europe and the high civilizations of Asia has many facets. The West and China and Japan share an interest in art produced for edification, meditation, and aesthetic enjoyment, in the representation of the human body and face, in the narrative theme, in nature and the mute objects of our daily life, in the individual artist's self-surrender and emotive experience. Such affinities are discussed in "Confrontations" and "Anticipations" in chapter 2. At the same time the difference of interpretation of similar themes East and West, as well as potential similarities of formal approaches embedded in different traditions, is thrown into relief.

A bird's-eye view of East-West relationships in the arts leaves hardly any doubt that Europe received more than it gave. Nor have foreign artistic invasions of Europe had as unfortunate results as the present Westernization of the Orient (see chapter 6). On the contrary, the ever quicker and shorter waves of European penetration of Near Eastern, Chinese, Egyptian, Japanese, Pacific, Negro, and Pre-Columbian cultures have been handled with supreme confidence by Western artists. Indeed, it was the uninterrupted contact of the West with non-European civilizations, particularly those of the Old World, that helped to foster the endless variety, vitality, and cosmopolitanism in our own art.

J. LEROY DAVIDSON:

Style—East and West

FEW OF US HAVE NOT HAD THE SURPRISING AND OFTEN PER-PLEXING EXPERIENCE OF SEEING A WORK OF ART—A PAINTING, A SCULPTURE, A BUILDING, PERHAPS EVEN A FRAGMENT OF A textile—which instantly conjured up memories of a host of other similar objects made by people living in vastly different areas of the world and in widely separated periods of time. Oddly enough, not many studies have been undertaken to find out why such startling similarities occur among the arts of different cultures and what their true relationship is. Occasionally, when those similarities appear to be quite evident they prove to be superficial. Obversely, objects that at first seem disparate, on closer examination, reveal a comparable or parallel point of view that relates them meaningfully to each other.

The totality of the visual elements that condition our reaction to a work of art is known as "style," and for convenience I shall use this term in an extremely broad sense. Style, in common usage, is confined to the formal analysis of a work of art, but at times in this discussion, for reasons that I hope will become clear, the term will also compre-hend subject matter. Although many categories of style have been established, none is ideal. Here I will use the conventional if inade-quate division of archaic, classic, mannerist, and baroque, but never with the connotation of their being cyclical.

Let us first consider the category of archaic as it applies to Greek sculpture of the seventh and sixth centuries B.C. Archaic figures char-acteristically are shown in a rigid frontal or side view, details are clearly articulated, planes are sharp and simple, drapery is flat and falls in systematic folds. When we survey the history of art we find this same syndrome of forms throughout most of pre-Ptolemaic Egypt, in much of European art from the sixth to the thirteenth century, in China in the fifth and sixth centuries, in most of Negro art in Africa, and in some early works of India.

It is no accident that these arts have common characteristics. In each instance they have grown out of a culture that was unquestioningly devoted to a religious ideal. Such mundane activities as war and trade continued, but each culture was imbued with a totality of belief. A figure was only as naturalistic as necessary to convey the fundamental significance of the god or man represented. A Buddhist living in China in the sixth century would see little strange in an archaic Greek statue or a Romanesque tympanum, but he might be mystified by a Sung landscape painted by one of his countrymen in the thirteenth century.

In classic periods forms are more naturalistic, less rigid, and more re-laxed; frontality and the vertical axis are replaced by the three-quarter view and the broken axis; landscape elements begin to appear. These features are dominant in the arts of Greece in the fifth century B.C., India in the fifth century A.D., China at the end of the sixth century, and Europe in the fifteenth century. The intensity of religion wanes during these periods; philosophy begins to conflict with faith; and an awakening interest in the physical world stimulates the beginnings of scientific attitudes. More emphasis is given to life on this earth than to some future existence. It is not that man has abandoned his beliefs, but that he was less overwhelmed by the immanence of divinity. We

1 Kore
Greek, 6th century B.C. (marble)
Acropolis Museum, Athens

2 Jizo
Japanese, 10th century A.D. (wood)
Art Museum, Princeton University

EXAMPLES OF
ARCHAIC STYLE

3 Sheikh el Beled
Egyptian, 2600 B.C. (wood)
Cairo Museum

4 The Victorious One
Jain, 9th century A.D. (sandstone)
Heeramaneck Collection, New York

Aphrodite   **5**
Greek, 4th century B.C. (marble)
Indiana University Art Museum, Bloomington

Buddha
Indian, Gupta period, 5th-6th century A.D. (stone)
Private Collection, U.S.A.   **6**

see changes not only in form but also in choice of subjects. Narrative elements intrude on religious themes and expand into a three-dimensional space. In China the Buddha figure appears in a measurable space. Similarly, the fifteenth-century Madonna moves out of her gold background into a setting. In Greece and in China the archaic conventions for drapery give way to the greater fluidity of soft cloth; in Italy Cimabue's schematic drapery is transformed first by Giotto, then more fully by Masaccio. Yet, what may appear as "naturalism" in classic art is quite abstract. Classic drapery, for instance, has no accidental folds to mar the perfection of a line, and the lineaments of the classic figure generally are typed rather than individualized.

The classic at times evolves imperceptibly toward the baroque—perhaps the most vague of all stylistic terms—and this is precisely what happened in Europe during the sixteenth and seventeenth centuries. Man was rapidly pursuing a course that had been launched by the intellectual explorations of the humanists during the Renaissance. Oriented toward science and philosophy, society was moving toward secularization and reacting in many areas to the tremendous commercial, political, and geographical expansion. This broadening of human horizons describes the cultural environment of the baroque style.

The most obvious characteristic of the baroque is an exuberance of forms accented by powerful contrasts of light and shade, as exemplified by Rubens, Bernini, and Caravaggio. But other artists of the same period, like Vermeer, with his restrained compositions and subtle lighting, or Poussin, whose designs are almost classic, are linked with Rubens and Caravaggio by an intensified naturalism, an attempt to exhaust ways by which to simulate the visual world.

The environment also affected the "style" of the artists' subject matter. The introduction of such innovations as genre, still life, and the landscape demonstrates the artist's increasing fascination with the world around him. Such probings into the nature of things reached a culmination in Rembrandt, whose portraits go beyond what is visually perceived to reveal the inner character of his subjects. This is the ultimate in realism. We find it also in Shakespeare's plays, but not, by contrast, in those by Marlowe, who emphasized the story and merely typed his characters.

When we look elsewhere, we find a baroque art in Europe in the late Antique and Roman worlds, in China in the eighth century, and in Japan in the thirteenth. In each country these were periods of religious confusion and conflict, a great deal of philosophical and scientific inquiry, and a formidable commercial expansion. We see tangible evidence of the baroque style in the exuberant façade of the early eighth-century Chinese shrine from the Nelson Gallery.

The baroque was not satisfied with the type portrait; every detail, down to the smallest mole, had to be shown, whether the subject was a Roman senator or a thirteenth-century Japanese monk. (It is not surprising, then, that one monk carved in a cave temple at Lung-mên, China, is affectionately known as Jim Farley.) The same attention to detail was lavished on drapery. The naturalistic folds of the classic tradition were re-examined and amplified by small accidental folds.

Textures were studied so that silk and wool, metal, and wood were distinctly defined. As Bernini tortured his marble to give versimilitude to his wig of Louis XIV, so the Japanese sculptor added glass eyes to his wood heads, and the Chinese stone carver emphasized the muscles and sinews of his guardians. While an early sixth-century Chinese guardian, abstracted and ideal, protects by virtue of his inherent power, during the seventh and eighth centuries these same guardians become menacing figures who give promise of protection by physical force, not by divine power.

The accepted period of mannerism in Europe is from about 1520 to 1560. Among the leading exponents in Italy were Bronzino, Portormo, Parmigianino, Giulio Romano, Giovanni da Bologna, and at times, Michelangelo. The style is characterized by elegant and attenuated figures whose postures are distinctly exaggerated and precariously arrested in motion. Space was distorted by abrupt and deep perspectives or a series of conflicting planes. All of these features indicate a rejection of canons that had been developed during the classic phase of the earlier Renaissance. Where the baroque artist built upon and further developed classic formulae, the mannerist discarded the traditions of his immediate predecessors.

Architectural design moved in the same direction. In Michelangelo's entrance to the Laurentian Library inset columns and consoles function as decorative motifs, not as supporting members, a contrivance that would have shocked an earlier generation. A triple staircase baffles the intruder and forces him to make a choice between a central onrushing cascade of curved steps, or one of the awkward stairs on either side. Giulio Romano in the Palazzo del Te in Mantua broke the straight line of his entablature by dropping every third triglyph in order to create an effect of instability.

The mannerists wrought changes not only in art forms but also in subject matter and content. Their women seem frigid, their men effeminate. Scenes of the macabre, like "Salome with the Head of John the Baptist," "Judith with the Head of Holofernes," and "The Suicide of Lucrece," were fashionable. Salacious, erotic, and pornographic works attained respectability. Giulio Romano was forced to leave Rome for making pornographic works; more significantly, he was soon able to return. Cranach in Germany made nude figures of Venus seem more naked by garnishing them with hats. The long-limbed, small-breasted beauties of Fontainebleau are blatantly erotic.

At the source of this art is a distinct malaise. Europe was torn by war. In 1527 Rome, the Holy City itself, was sacked. Ten years earlier, Martin Luther had shattered the cohesion of the Universal Church. Philosophic speculations and scientific discoveries were creating problems rather than resolving them. Columbus had opened up a new concept of the world. The artists and the elite could not be satisfied with the past. Mannerism is an art of the extreme and the neurotic. We should not be surprised that as a style mannerism was not emphasized until about 1920, when men found themselves living in a civilization emerging from a great war and facing the shattering impact of Communism and Freud.

7 Bodhisattva
Chinese, Sui dynasty, 6th century A.D. (stone)
The Metropolitan Museum of Art, New York

The Veiled Lady, by Raphael
Italian, 16th century (oil painting)
Florence, Pitti Palace

8

9
A Roman Emperor
Greco-Roman, 2nd century (marble)
The Metropolitan Museum of Art

10
Guardian Divinity (detail)
Chinese, T'ang period, 8th century (stone)
William Rockhill Nelson Gallery, Kansas City

Like all styles, mannerism reflects and at the same time helps mold its culture. Martin Luther, Columbus, and Copernicus helped create the condition for mannerism, but their actions were permitted only because of circumstances at a particular moment in history. The explosion of ideas created an unease which was not quieted until another generation was able to adapt itself to the new world its parents had discovered. The twentieth century has endured a similar shock, and perhaps the increasing crescendo of new styles is a sign of mannerism in our time.

Mannerism manifests itself elsewhere in the world during periods of drastic change. In Egypt, for instance, new religious institutions established by Akhenaten disrupted an archaic tradition that had continued longer than any other in history, and mannerism in the arts soon followed the theological revolution. When the old religion was restored, the arts reverted to their archaic pattern and maintained it until traditional beliefs were undermined by intellectual encounters with the classic world.

During India's period of mannerism in the tenth and eleventh centuries, artist-craftsmen in certain areas (such as Khajuraho) parted with tradition. Like their European counterparts who lived 500 years later, they created an incredible human figure by pulling and twisting it and entwining it upon itself. These elongated and artificially posturing bodies often have a singular elegance, but lack the quality of living, breathing flesh and blood and the extraordinary vitality that had been India's artistic legacy for more than three thousand years. The

11
Louis XIV, by Bernini
Italian, 17th century (marble)
Versailles

12
Dancing Figure
Indian, 7th century (sandstone)
Private Collection, U.S.A.

full-breasted female deities with small waists, broad hips, and massive thighs were turned into frozen images of courtly grace with slender limbs and too perfect hemispherical breasts. As Cranach changed Venus into a courtesan, the Indian sculptor transformed the descendants of ancient mother goddesses into the concubines of a Raja's harem.

As in the later European mannerist period, eroticism accompanied this change in style. Figures in fantastically complex and perverse association were carved in conspicuous places on temple walls. Such license corresponded with that of the Tantric cults flourishing simultaneously in the Indian middle ages. The ritual of these cults included the drinking of spirituous liquors, eating of fish and meat and, at times, the performance of the sexual act, practices as shocking to the Hindu then as they are to many of them today. Tantric cults and their excesses bear the same relationship to Indian religion as sculpture in the eleventh century to the earlier art of India. The immediate source of erotica was Tantracism, but Tantra itself may be considered a manneristic form of religion.

China's unique expression of mannerism is more difficult to detect. The style developed in the sixteenth century from the innovations of a group of elite painters that included the painter, Hsü Wei, and critic-painter Tung Ch'i-ch'ang among its leaders. Hsü Wei, with his seemingly careless "ink-flinging," moved in one direction. Tung, giving lip service to tradition, moved in another by distorting forms and spatial relationships. Combining the two approaches, others used

13
Saint Peter
French, 12th century (stone relief)
Moissac, Cathedral

14
Surasundari
Indian, Khajuraho style, 11th century (sandstone)
Denver Art Museum

14

violent brushwork to effect abrupt spatial transitions. Unknowingly, but for the same basic reasons, these artists were relating to their society just as the European mannerists had a generation earlier.

The sixteenth century in China had seen almost total corruption at the Ming court, which had fallen under the domination of the eunuchs. Many of the leading intellectuals rejected their traditional role in China, avoided the court, and retired in provincial seclusion. Informal gatherings, that brought together Tung Ch'i-ch'ang, Hsü Wei, and the theoretician Mo Shih-lung, were, in effect, ingrown self-admiration societies detached from the mainstream of Chinese life. They nurtured eccentricities and turned to the arts as a means of expression. Like the European mannerists, their procedures were intellectual and analytical. They looked to art rather than to nature for their inspiration. It is significant that both Tung Ch'i-ch'ang in China and Vasari in Italy are remembered more for their aesthetic commentaries than for their paintings.

I have stressed mannerism here because its mode of expression has been more varied than those of the archaic, the classic, or the baroque. Since mannerism is essentially the neurotic rejection of an immediately preceding tradition, each instance of the style is manifested and recognizable only within the framework of its historical sequence. The style takes different shape when reacting against an archaic style as in Egypt, a classic style as in Europe, and a baroque style as in China. In our own time, a painting of a flag by Jasper Johns, with all its simple naturalism, may be interpreted as mannerist—no less than Robert Rauschenberg's eccentric "painting" of a bed—because it represents a

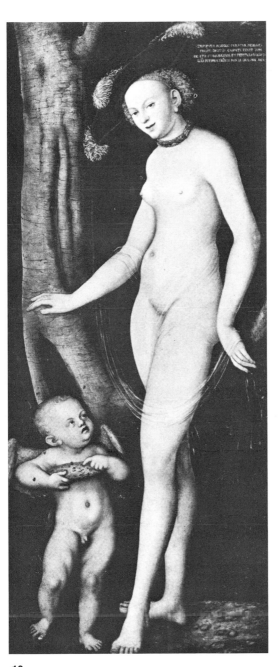

15
Buddha or Bodhisattva
Chinese, Northern Wei period, 6th century (stone)
Museum of Fine Arts, Boston

complete rejection of all accepted contemporary art forms.

If we concede that there is a relationship between neurosis and mannerism, we will have to concede that the cultural environments that spawned mannerism were basically neurotic. The mannerist artist, however, is not necessarily a neurotic. The forms he created and the subjects he chose were inevitably what his acute sensitivity as an artist was able to register as the requirements of his time.

To reach a fundamental understanding of the determinants of any style is a formidable task. We can at least collect whatever facts about a culture are available, but in correlating the individual pieces of information, the pitfall lies in what we regard as a cause and what we regard as an effect. An interesting, and in some ways amusing example of the interrelationship of cultural factors comes from seventh-century China. The Empress Wu had usurped the throne. By her order, a Buddhist sutra was invented, and in this forged scripture Maitreya, the future Buddha, was destined to rule China as a woman. At times this T'ang Empress was dressed as Maitreya while she enjoyed illicit affairs with the more attractive monks of the country. This episode tells us something about the religious attitudes of the period if not about the baroque style then flourishing in Buddhist art. It was, in fact, symptomatic of the practical and worldy condition of the religion, in itself a part of the cultural syndrome.

Such incidents support our conclusions about the relationship of a style to its period, even though they may not reveal the underlying causes that mold the psychological configuration of a culture. A single anecdote, of course, is not enough evidence. Happily, in this case,

16
Venus and Amor, by L. Cranach the Elder
German, 16th century (tempera)
Borghese Gallery, Rome

T'ang China offers abundant documentation that sustains the interpretation suggested by this one episode. Written records, however, are not always available and, even when they are, they may contain conscious or unintentional distortions of facts. Only a work of art stands as an unequivocal witness of its time.

The study of comparative styles is eminently worthwhile, perhaps even essential in our integrating world; it enables us, by inductive reasoning, to reach unfamiliar levels of understanding. Inconographic analyses are essential, of course, but in addition, particularly at this time, a refined method for analysis of comparative style is needed. With this tool the historian of literature and music as well as the art historian could accomplish what Professor Panofsky has with iconography in his brilliant study of Dürer, which plumbs the mind and resources of a great artist. We cannot achieve this now, but at least we can span time and space in an attempt to understand the universal human quality of art. We should be able to recognize that the differences between Europe and Asia are differences only of idiom; that many Asian art forms of the past would be more intelligible to our European ancestors than to Asians living today; that most of us now would feel at home in the atmosphere of T'ung Ch'i-ch'ang or Bronzino; that the Chinese sculptor working on the cave temples at Yun Kang would find few artistic barriers between himself and a fellow craftsman of an archaic Greek *kouros* or a tympanum on the cathedral at Vézelay.

FOR FURTHER READING

J. L. Davidson, "Mannerism and Neurosis in the Erotic Art of India," *Oriental Art,* n.s. 6, n.3, pp. 82-90 (Autumn, 1960).

M. Schapiro, "Style," in *Anthropology Today, an Encyclopedic Inventory,* 1953, pp. 287-312.

17
Stately Trees and Mountain Peaks, by Tung Ch'i-Ch'ang
Chinese, 1555-1636 (painting on silk)
Museum of Fine Arts, Boston

Confrontations
and Far-Eastern Anticipations

CONFRONTATIONS

THE DIFFERENCES AND THE PARALLELS OR AFFINITIES BETWEEN ARTISTIC MODES OF EXPRESSION DESCRIBED IN THE PRECEDING CHAPTER ARE ESSENTIALLY METAPHYSICAL. THE COMPARISONS can be extended to other problems of style affected by theme and subject matter, techniques, and other practical considerations. The artist's vision, his ways of interpreting and his manner of expressing his perceptions are also relevant to such stylistic comparisons.

One type of analysis is investigated in Benjamin Rowland's *Art in the East and West.* He takes a number of standard themes such as the male nude, the female nude, and the divine image, and by confronting an Eastern and a Western treatment of each, he is able to draw all sorts of striking and illuminating inferences and conclusions. The method followed in the first part of this chapter is directly inspired by that book, some of the categories and illustrations being identical; in some cases Rowland's text has been paraphrased and shortened, but this is not to imply that he should in any way be held responsible for statements made here. The interested reader is urged to consult his very stimulating book.

18
Seishi Bosatsu
Japanese, 11th century (color on silk)
Benjamin Rowland Collection, Cambridge, Massachusetts

THE MYSTIC IDEAL

A fundamental affinity of artistic intent between the Italian panel ascribed to Paolo Veneziano and the temple painting on silk by an unidentified artist of the Fujiwara period transcends their differences in technique, style, and actual subject matter.

A *Bosatsu* or Bodhisattva, in the context of the Buddhist sect which inspired this particular work, is a quasi-divine figure without any experience of an earlier human existence, just one step removed from becoming a divinity in its own right. The artist, therefore, intends to endow him with an innately transcendent beauty. Saint Ursula, on the other hand, is definitely a transmuted human. The painter heightens her natural beauty, for which she was famous, with a background of gold leaf that suggests

19
Saint Ursula, by Paolo Veneziano
Italian, 14th century
Indiana University Art Museum

infinitely luminous space, similar to the celestial atmosphere in which the *Bosatsu* floats. The Japanese work is close to being an icon, that is to say, an image possessing a magic and sacred nature, but the picture of the saint, for all her acquired status as a "bride of Christ," really belongs in the category of "reminders." Stylistically, the fluid, linear manner of the Eastern figure contrasts with the heavier and more monumental character of the Western representative. But in spite of iconographic and stylistic differences, both images convey a sense of unearthly grace and ineffable beauty, and each work either sets or follows a standard of aristocratic perfection of form representative of the culture from which it springs.

20

Portrait of a Gentleman, by Thomas de Keyser
Dutch, 17th century
Collection of Mr. and Mrs. Albert Elsen, Bloomington

21

Ogotai
Ch'ien Lung period, 1736-1795, (From an album of Portraits of 24 Chinese Emperors)
The Metropolitan Museum of Art, Gift of Mrs. Edward S. Harkness, 1947

THE FORMAL PORTRAIT

The art of portraiture has been more fully developed in the West than in the East, in part because of the importance of the individual in the Western tradition. Portraits, especially of rulers, are not unknown in China, but tend to limn an idea of a sovereign whose physical aspects are not appreciably different from his predecessors or successors. The clearly individualized portrait of Ogotai, reproduced here, is something of an exception in Chinese art; only in the portraits memorializing famous Ch'an abbots does the Chinese artist attempt what might be defined as a psychological commentary on his model. Though not as subtle or revelatory, this portrait belongs in that tradition of great likenesses painted during the Sung period.

We know very little about either Ogotai or the Dutch gentleman. The third son and chosen successor of Genghiz Khan, Ogotai reigned from 1229 to 1241. He consolidated his father's conquests, and was eventually succeeded by his nephew Kublai. Historically he is remembered as very intelligent, commonsensical and "solid," good-natured, jovial, extremely generous and inclined toward clemency, and a heavy drinker. We probably do not know

very much more about his personality, therefore, than did the painter who was commissioned some five hundred years after his death to paint his portrait, but we may nonetheless accept the representation as a valid one. It fits all our preconceived notions about the physical features of this particular Mongolian ruler, and in this we are at one with the Chinese of Ch'ien Lung's time.

The European gentleman who sat for Thomas de Keyser in the seventeenth century is even more of a mystery. Is he a Dutch burgher, an English buccaneer, a German princeling *incognito?* No matter who he may be, he appears to us as sure of his power and rank as Ogotai, and as accustomed to being obeyed as the Emperor.

Both subjects have that slightly *désabusé* look which men in high positions sometimes reveal to the artist for whom they sit. Since we know no more about the Dutch painter than we do about the Chinese, however, we are saved from making irrelevant speculations and tendentious interpretations based on the theory that a portrait always tells more about the painter than about the sitter.

Mother and Child   **22**
Khajuraho, about 11th century (sandstone carving)
Hope Collection, Bloomington

MOTHER AND CHILD

The Western artist has created endless variations on
the theme of the Madonna holding the Blessed
Child—emphasizing mother love, sacred wonder,
infinite tenderness, and other comparable emotions,
and using a wide range of poses. This French sculptor has happily combined the required sense of
virginal purity, reflected in the Mother's face, with
the firmness with which she must balance the heavy
Child on her protruding left hip. Any physical crud-
ity and effort is effectively disguised by the play of
drapery, and modesty is necessarily preserved.

The Indian sculpture shows a mother holding her
infant in an almost identical posture. There is nothing sacred about this image, however, even though
it was carved on the façade of a temple. In a land
where fertility in all its aspects is a prime motive of
art as well as of religious belief, maternity is in no

Virgin and Child   **23**
French, 13th century (polychrome plaster)
Hope Collection

way exalted. While the iconography of the nativity
of the Buddha bears some slight resemblance to the
Christian tradition, Buddha's mother is rarely portrayed in the act of holding him to be worshipped.
In any event, the sculpture represented here is not a
Buddhist but a Jain work. Jainism, an abstruse doctrine, had no use for images, at least for those that
seemed to glorify the fruitfulness of life. The specific
motivation for this work remains a puzzle, which
can be explained historically by the effect of Brahmanism on Jainism. The figures on the Jain temples
in Khajuraho show the same sensuality characteristic
of the figures on the Brahmanistic temples. This contradiction of the essential asceticism of the Jain religion can be explained only on grounds of propin-
quity to the Brahmanistic places of worship.

THE MALE NUDE

Kubera, in Indian mythology, is the King of the Yakshas, or male fertility divinities, and also God of Wealth and Regent of the North. While corpulence is traditionally associated with rank and authority in India, the pot-bellied aspect of this minor god is due rather to yogic insufflation or *prana,* which fills his body. A sense of material and spiritual well-being is conveyed in the standard manner by suggesting the heaviness of flesh and muscular tension. The artist makes no attempt at illusionistic realism by disguising the nature of the stone with which he works.

The Greco-Roman torso of a somewhat younger man might conceivably represent a young Hermes or Hercules rather than an ephebus. The superficial resemblance between this and the Indian sculpture is very intriguing, but the differences are more significant than the similarities. The polished marble is clearly intended to simulate the smoothness of flesh, and the re-creation of the body is strongly anatomical. Unlike the Indian sculpture, this classical torso is in no way symbolic.

24
25

24
Torso of Kubera
Central India, 10th-11th century (light sandstone)
Frank Caro Collection, New York

25
Torso of a Youth
Greco-Roman, period undetermined (marble)
Indiana University Art Museum

The Last Judgment   **26**
Persian, Safavid period, 15th-16th centuries (miniature painting)
Philip Hofer Collection, Cambridge

HELL

The startling similarity between two Infernal Rulers, each presiding over the punishment of evil-doers and each shown in the act of devouring especially odious sinners, implies either that the Buddhist influenced the Christian artist, which is not probable, or that they are both indebted to a common tradition, also shared by .the Mohammedans. There are close parallels at the opposite end of the scale, in the Paradises: a Sienese *Maestà*, with Christ enthroned among the Saints and the Seraphim, an

Ajanta fresco showing the Buddha in majesty, surrounded by Bodhisattvas, Arhats, and Lokapalas, and Mohammed's Paradise, where Allah is a flame and his principal acolytes are veiled, show a striking affinity with one another. Two works will serve as a useful introduction to the entire question: H. Sunderland's *Islam and the Divine Comedy*, 1926, and J. J. L. Duyvendak's article, "A Chinese Divina Commedia," in *T'oung Pao*, xli (1952), pp. 255-316.

27

The God of Heavenly Punishment

From a 13th century painting reproduced in Japanese
Scroll Paintings, *vol. 6, by S. Ienaga, 1960.*

The Inferno according to Dante
Florentine, 15th century (engraving attributed to Baldini)
National Gallery of Art, Washington, D. C., Rosenwald Collection

Herd Boy Washing His Buffalo
Northern Sung period (painting on silk)
Frank Caro Collection

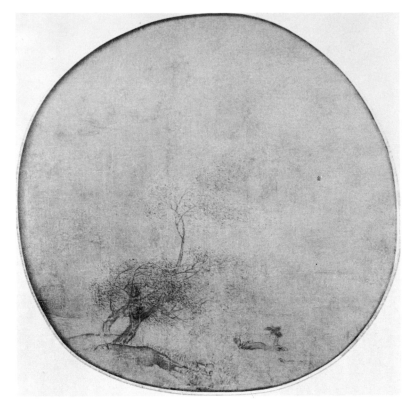

29

THE IMPRESSIONISTIC LANDSCAPE

By 1830 Sainte-Beuve had helped to propagate the idea, dear to the Romantics, that a landscape was a "state of the soul." The artist must strive to communicate an essence, ineffable by nature and poetic by definition, to be found in a corner of Nature where man's presence was not predominant.

In effect, the Taoist painter in China had long been working in this mode, or something very close to it. After establishing a given mood, the painting should stimulate philosophic reflection. For the Chinese painter this meant spending unlimited time in contemplation before nature, and then painting at home. Such distillation of experience fits very closely Wordsworth's prescription for a poem: "emotion recollected in tranquility."

Corot, on the other hand, was one of the first of the *plein air* practitioners, who communicate the essence of an experience immediately and spontaneously; by contrast with the Chinese, he is a simple man, not much given to metaphysical rumination.

It should be noted that the Chinese painting illustrated here has added connotations derived from the Ch'an Buddhist symbolism of Child and Buffalo.

30

Le Fort Détaché, by J. B. C. Corot
French, 1796-1865 (cire glacée)
Indiana University Art Museum

Sea and Mountain Landscape,
by Kano Tsunenobu
Japanese, about 1700
Indiana University Art Museum

THE EXPRESSIONISTIC LANDSCAPE

31

32

One is tempted to equate Marin's turbulent and energetic handling of his brush with the broken-ink style developed by the Chinese masters and codified in Japan by the leaders of the Kano School. The small landscape by Tsunenobu is perfectly representative of the Eastern manner: the essential elements of a scene are presented, with economical energy, in relation to one another. Every part is clear, and there is no ambiguity whatever in the picture. In all but his very best works, Marin tends to be confusing if not downright fuzzy. He works by a series of splashes and slashes; sometimes there are happy strikes. Clearly he feels strongly about the sea, but this little water-color indicates that he is not fully in control of his technique of expression. His brush strokes have no individual character, and the meaning of the geometrical forms in the foreground and on the left is uncertain.

Composed from My House, by John Marin
American, 1870-1953 (water-color)
Collection of the Herron Museum of Art,
Indianapolis

33

Theatre Street, by Okumura Masanobu
Japanese, 1690-1768 (woodblock print)
Robert Laurent Collection, Bloomington

THE FLEETING MOMENT

Totally unknown to one another, at opposite ends
of the Eurasian continent, the Japanese artist and
the Frenchman pursued an identical goal—to capture the essence of a particular moment, the flavor
of a given place, the elements of which would never
reform themselves in precisely the same patterns.
The Japanese called this kind of temporal impression
by the poetic term *Ukiyo-e*, the "Fleeting World,"
but the concept was not unknown in the West. The
primary intent of the genre painters such as Teniers
was also to capture a mood, though they may have
had other motives such as satire, not always a dis-
cernable part of the Japanese treatment.

Debucourt reveals the world of fashion and the
ladies of the *demi-monde* of Paris mingling under

34
La Promenade Publique,
by Philibert Debucourt
French, 1755-1832 (aquatint)
Courtesy of the Art Institute of Chicago

the chestnut trees of the gardens of the Palais-Royal. The year is 1792, when it was still possible to enjoy life with a sense of recklessness, an atmosphere that was soon rudely interrupted by the Terror. This elegant work is therefore an unique historical document as well, and a social commentary. The Palais-Royal still stands, but it is inhabited by ghosts.

Masanobu also informs us very precisely about the look of the Edo townsfolk of 1730, who are as evanescent as the Frenchmen of the other print. Moreover, he has caught something of the feeling of a bustling Japanese crowd intent on having a good time, a colorful mood which even today captivates visitors to any modern amusement district such as Asakusa in Tokyo.

Golden Crowned Wagtail, by J. J. Audubon

From the Elephant Folio edition, The Birds of America, *1827-1838 (colored lithograph from a painting)*
Lilly Rare Book Library, Indiana University

35

Wagtail Bird

Early Ming dynasty, 14th century (painting on silk)
Benjamin Rowland Collection

36

BIRDS

At first blush Audubon seems to be all scientific accuracy and the Chinese artist entirely imbued with poetic truth. This, however, is a false dichotomy, since these values can be held in harmony with one another in a single work of art.

The Chinese bird is very carefully observed, both in its form and plumage and in its relation to its immediate surroundings, but as in all good Chinese painting regardless of ostensible subject matter, the work is endowed with a sense of life. In short, this is rhythmic vitality expressed by a highly decorative representative.

Is this sense of vitality missing in Audubon's birds? Not at all. He went after his subjects in almost precisely the same way the Chinese painter did: he identified himself with them. Springing from a totally different tradition, he achieves something of the same end since he too is really seeking the essential, vital, expressive meaning of his theme.

Sea Shells and Prawns on a Leaf
Northern Sung dynasty, ca. 11th century (painting on silk)
Courtesy of Frank Caro

Eggs and Napkin, by William Bailey
Contemporary American (drawing)
Hope Collection

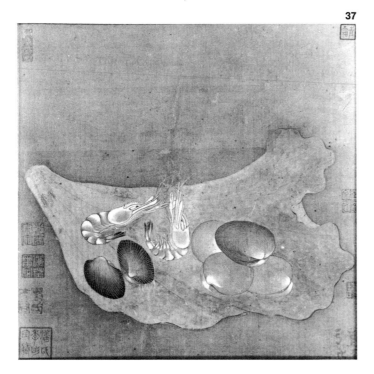

37

38

STILL LIFE

Since Cézanne, still life has been a mode of exploring forms, colors, textures, spatial relationships, surface and inner tensions, and other plastic problems. The artist approaches the social, philosophic, esoteric, or physiological aspects of the objects under examination as existential phenomena, and his method is closer to that of the scientist than to the poet's. In terms of white on white Bailey has placed his eggs on a rumpled napkin, a table being suggested rather than indicated, and his composition immediately suggests a landscape. A monumental quality is imparted to objects which in themselves are brittle or soft, and the simple drawing has the clean lines of a geometrical demonstration. But we have not left the the realm of essences—"Euclid alone has looked on Beauty bare"—and the Western and Chinese artist meet on common ground. The Oriental cannot understand the connotations of "still life" or *nature morte*, since life is never still and Nature never dies. He approaches his prawns and his shells and his curling leaf as living entities undergoing a constant process; his explorations are of the spiritual implications of this grouping of natural forms. He does not express himself in abstract terms, but we can see that he has to solve the same kind of plastic problems that the Westerner faces, by identical graphic means. According to Chinese aesthetic theory, the ultimate level of meaning of the Sung work is symbolic and metaphysical; the same yardstick applied to Bailey's drawing proves that it too is suffused with that "rhythmic vitality" which the Chinese regard as the beginning and end of art.

39

Fish and Rocks, by Chu Ta (Pa-ta Shan-jen)
Chinese, ca. 1625-1700
The John M. Crawford, Jr., Collection, New York

FORMAL ABSTRACTION

Fish swimming with unrestrained freedom about two rocks, apparently suspended in mid-air, are the ostensible subject of this work. At a profounder level the painting is a measure of the ability of the painter-poet to understand and express the pleasure of the fish in terms of his own pleasure in watching them.

Here everything is abstracted—water, land, light, surface realism. There is simply essential form and movement, yet nothing is missing. It is abstractionism at the service of an emotion, or an idea.

ANTICIPATIONS

The following passage in James Cahill's book on Chinese painting suggested the method followed in the second part of this chapter:

The quality of a painting reflects the personal quality of the artist; its expressive content derives from his mind, and has no necessary relationship to anything the artist or the viewer thinks or feels about the object represented. The value of the picture does not depend upon its likeness to anything in nature. The object in nature serves as raw material which must be transformed into an artistic idiom, and the mode of this transformation, the character of the lines and forms produced by the brush, reveals something about the person who drew them, and about his mood at the moment he drew them. "Anyone who talks about painting in terms of likeness," writes Su Tung-p'o, "deserves to be classed with the children." All this seems precocious in relation to Occidental art theory, anticipating ideas which did not appear in the West until well in the nineteenth century. . . . [pp. 89-91]

Not only was there a gap of some eight hundred years between the time these ideas began to appear in China and the period of Western development of the same concepts, but there is no probability that the Eastern artists influenced the Westerners. Merely to point up Chinese precocity in matters which stir Western artists deeply today would be an insufficient reason to illustrate such anticipations here. There is another and crucial factor. Certain critics, Sir Herbert Read among others, have stated that Western artists have reached the limits of painting, and that they have every reason now to look to their Eastern predecessors, whose values as well as techniques and perceptions may turn out to be not at all bizarre and unfamiliar. These earlier Eastern artists may therefore suggest paths leading to a rebirth of painting in the West. It is even possible that an aesthetic language common to both East and West might be evolved.

The categories and examples used in this part of the chapter were suggested by *Some Contemporary Elements in Classical Chinese Art* by Tseng Yu-ho.

41

Lily, by Li Shan

Chinese, early 18th century
The Art Institute of Chicago, S. M. Nickerson Fund

LINEAR ABSTRACTION

Expressiveness sacrifices realistic detail to stress the major visual truths of a plant observed at a particular stage of its life. Even a botanist might agree that this rhythmic pattern of curving lines tells us much about the response of the lily to its environment, and the moralist will not fail to transpose the theme into a human context. That the composition is a harmonious one is our good luck; the work was not conceived as a piece of decoration but as an exercise in analyzing nature. Would Klee and Hartung agree?

40

The Serene Bank of the Hsiang River, by Hsia Ch'ang

Chinese, 1388-1470 (figure detail from a landscape scroll)
The William Rockhill Nelson Gallery of Art (Nelson Fund)

VISUAL PARTICIPATION

In the standard Chinese landscape—especially in the long vertical scrolls—the onlooker is supposed to be a member of that tiny group of men who are traveling through it and to whom its elements are increasingly revealed as they progress along the carefully marked paths. In this horizontal scroll by a painter of the Ming dynasty the venue is changed; the artist's use of a scale closer to the human's suggests that he had little desire to stress man's puniness in relation to the immensity of nature. The onlooker is brought right into the picture plane. A few more steps and he will be at the edge of the rock above the river, or else he will bump into the bamboo. The elimination of top and bottom edges has the effect of bringing the middle distance very close and of suppressing the background almost entirely. Another curious effect, created by the simplest of devices, is the intense luminosity of the water.

42

Juro, The God of Longevity, by Hakuin
Japanese, 1685-1768 (sumi on paper)
Collection of Ulfert Wilke, New York

ACTION PAINTING

One way of defining action painting stresses the unorthodox approach, that is to say, the untrammeled and apparently uncontrolled use of materials, the splashing of color on canvas or paper, with an evident premium on results that are accidental or automatic. There are many examples of famous Chinese eccentrics who may be legitimate protoypes of Mathieu or Pollock.

The other approach, while apparently just as unconventional, is considerably more rational and surer of the end it wishes to attain. The Ch'an or Zen painter, who has trained himself most rigorously, has such a tight control of his brush and his ink that his statement has the spontaneity and energy of lightning. He communicates that moment of truth, that flash of intuition, tantamount to revelation, which the Japanese call *satori*. There can be nothing accidental about it; in a sense the painter must undergo a life-long preparation for the moment when that bolt of lightning will strike him; the painting then becomes truly emotion recollected in excitement.

The Zen artist, who is never an eccentric, has another tool at his disposal—calligraphy. In a typical Zen painting the boundary between image and ideogram tends to disappear. The strokes in each echo one another, forming a continuous composition, and are equally informative. The artist's entire being has been transfused into his brush.

43

Mountain Landscape, by Wang Hui
Chinese, 1632-1717
Frank Caro Collection

POINTILLISME

The use of small horizontal brush-strokes or parallel ink spots instead of lines goes back to Mi Fei, who lived in the latter part of the eleventh century. The method is not dependent on the juxtaposition of carefully selected patches of color that will become fused in the eye of the beholder, in obedience to the law of "simultaneous contrast" discovered by Chevreul and applied by Seurat and Signac, among others. The Chinese apply frequent dark patches on a lighter area, which is still damp, so that the ink runs a little. Contours soften and the landscape created seems drenched in mist—all for the purpose of conveying a mood.

In this painting by Wang Hui the solid columns, which define the mountains, are treated with a kind of reverse abstractionism: all angular outlines are blurred and only volume is stressed.

43

绿　垂
々　柳
帶　下
雨　春
耕　水
破　滿
一　田
縷　農
煙　失
　　寒
石
濤

44　Landscape with Buffalo, by Shih-T'ao

Chinese, 1703
The Art Institute of Chicago,
Kate S. Buckingham Fund

TACHISME

The invention of the *p'o-mo* or broken ink technique, ascribed to the eighth-century painter, Wang Wei, marks a major turning point in the history of Chinese painting. Ch'an or Zen painters particularly favored this style since it implied the use of rapid but highly controlled strokes, dots, and ink splashes to record the artist's sudden perception of a significant visual truth. The revelation needed to be stated most expressively, at the expense of careful delineation of form. Detail, explicitness of location, and other data are regarded as irrelevant. The successful use of this technique depends on long training in observation of nature, constant practice in calculating the amounts of water and ink to be splashed, and strict control of arm and wrist. Speed of execution is thus a function of years of schooling, so that nothing might be left to chance or accident.

Western tachists like Jackson Pollock and Tapié proclaim their indebtedness to this as well as other aspects of "action painting," in which the immediacy of the artist's involvement in his statement is stressed. The question is how much Pollock's compositions depend on irrational or accidental coincidences. By comparison, the Chinese painter is highly rational and selective—and never obscure, puzzling or merely decorative in an anarchic kind of way.

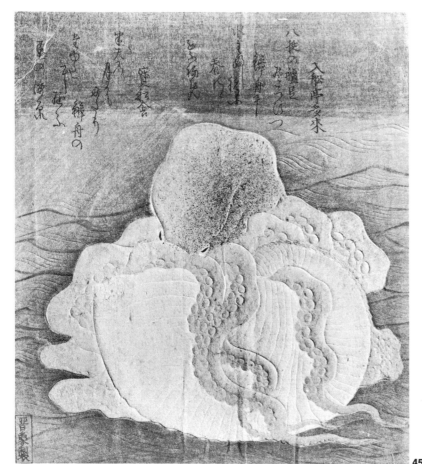

八杯再多来
蛮々の糟と
辯舟の
を乃陽民
虫天ら
さゆ々に
まゆ不になふ
馬り海ら私

45

Octopus and Nautilus, by Shinsho

Japanese, 19th century (surimono)
The Art Institute of Chicago

SURREALISM

Surrealism is a mode capable of many definitions. Forms produced by both the association and the dissociation of ideas, by that kind of hybridization called metamorphosis or transformation, and by all kinds of controlled and uncontrolled imaginings, are encountered in the Orient almost from the beginning. The East is equally familiar with the surrealism of dreams and hallucinations which modern psychologists explore. The poem which inspired this illustration reads, "The octopus floating upon the field of the sea is like the moon in mid-sky." Here form is not distorted; natural processes are not restructured in some fantastic way. All elements of the work are possible in nature, yet "other-worldly" seems the only cogent adjective for this image.

46

Winter

Ch'ing dynasty, 18th century (a decorative marble picture)
William Rockhill Nelson Gallery of Art (Nelson Fund)

OBJET TROUVÉ

Modernists make much of the fact that certain objects clearly not made by man seem to justify Oscar Wilde's dictum that Nature imitates Art. This idea occurred to the Chinese long ago, but it is doubtful whether they attached as much aesthetic significance to this kind of happy accident as we do.

Peppers, by Chih Pai Chih

Chinese, 19th-20th century
Frank Caro Collection

CONTROLLED DESIGN

"Design"—that vast area of artistic activity which embraces everything beyond the formal modes of expression but which traditionally referred to the restrictive category of ornament or decoration—is clearly in great debt to the Far East. Oriental ideas of composition, perspective, spatial relationships and respect for materials and textures historically have been important to the development of design in the West. Communication rather than embellishment is the operative principle for the Eastern artist, and economy of statement, where restraint and directness reinforce pungency, has become the first value for the Western designer. He has a message to deliver, and though one might argue that it is not the disinterested one of a "pure" painter, both designer and painter want to communicate in the same way. The more tightly organized the design, therefore, the more distinct the message.

The Chinese and Japanese are accomplished in the several ways of achieving pungency. This painting by Chih Pai Chih is an extraordinarily and ferociously concentrated statement of all the sensory connotations and implications of a familiar vegetable. And, at the same time, its blend of the pictorial with the calligraphic lends an admirably decorative quality to the painting.

FOR FURTHER READING

James Cahill, *Chinese Painting*, 1960.

Chinese Calligraphy and Painting in the Collection of John M. Crawford, Jr., 1962.

Thomas Munro, *Oriental Esthetics*, 1965.

Sir Herbert Read, "The Limits of Painting," *Studio International Art* (January, 1964).

B. Rowland, *Art in the East and West*, 1954, and 1964 (paperback).

M. Tapié and T. Haga, *Avant-Garde Art in Japan*, 1962.

Tseng Yu-ho, *Some Contemporary Elements in Classical Chinese Art*, 1963.

Le Paysage en Orient et en Occident, catalogue of an exhibition held at the Louvre in 1960.

III

Cultural Diffusion from An-Yang to the Danube:
The Role of the Eurasian Steppe

WILLIAM SAMOLIN:

FOR SOME FOUR MILLENNIA THE EURASIAN STEPPE HAS TO A VARYING DEGREE LINKED EAST AND WEST. THIS ENORMOUS BELT OF TERRITORY LIES GENERALLY BETWEEN THE FORTY-FIFTH AND fiftieth parallels of north latitude extending from Hungary on the west to the borders of Manchuria on the east. Massive mountain ranges isolate portions of this belt but are not insuperable obstacles against military operations. The mountains do restrict the nomadic movement of the transhumance.

The unaccidented grassland of the steppe proper undergoes long periods of summer drought, a characteristic of continental climate. Removed from the tempering influence of the sea, the Eurasian steppe region fluctuates between extremes of burning heat in summer and bitter cold in winter. Only the toughest humans and animals can survive under these conditions and both men and beasts become resourceful and adaptable.

The term Eurasian, which is not too common in the United States where it has a special connotation, suggests a view of Europe as a mere extension of Asia. The Ural Mountains, traditionally regarded as the boundary between Europe and Asia, are really a system of badly eroded wooded hills, similar to the Appalachians of the eastern United States. Only to the extreme north do the Urals reach altitudes of over five thousand feet; in the south, they gradually disappear into the steppe, leaving a wide uninterrupted corridor.

The steppe belt is bounded on the north by a forest belt, the East European and Siberian taiga, which has had considerable effect on the economy and ethnology of the steppe population. To the south the steppe extends to the shores of the Black Sea, the foothills of the Caucasus, the shores of the Caspian Sea, the desert of Ust Urt between the Caspian and Aral seas, the northern shores of the Aral Sea, the Syr Darya (the Jaxartes of old), which flows into the Aral, and finally to the Central Asian mountain masses. The steppe skirts the range of the Qara Tau, a northwestern spur of the great T'ien Shan system. Here it is broken by the spurs of the T'ien Shan into compartments which extend into the taiga and the tundra beyond. One compartment consists of the Ili and Balkash basins, the other, lying beyond the Djungarski Ala Tau and the Tarbaghatai, forms the southwestern portion of Djungaria. The Djungarian compartment is separated from Mongolia by the great ancient range of the Altai, the Chin Shan or "Golden Mountain" of the Chinese.

The Altai range, running roughly northwest and southeast, serves as the western boundary of Mongolia, which is surrounded by mountains on three sides; to the south, Mongolia borders on the Yellow River (Huang Ho) plain. Mongolia proper includes a northern and southern grass belt. The center is a gobi, not a true desert but rather a dusty scrub growth region such as the North American Southwest, and thus is not altogether uninhabitable. The "gobi people," as they are known, do not, however, lead as affluent a life as their relatives in the true grassland.

The eastern terminus of the Eurasian steppe may be set at the western borders of Manchuria, a region delimited by the Ta Khingan (Great

48
Cheekpiece: Horse in Flying Gallop
Caucasian, 12th to 9th century B.C.
Heeramaneck Collection

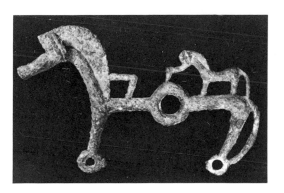

49
Cheekpiece: Small Horse Standing on the Back of Another
Etruscan or Caucasian, 8th century B.C. or earlier
Indiana University Art Museum

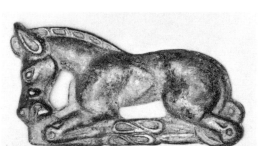

50
Plaque: Crouching Horse
Ordos, 7th century B.C. or later
Heeramaneck Collection

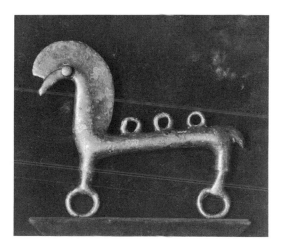

51
Cheekpiece: Horse
Caucasian, 10th century B.C.
Heeramaneck Collection

Note: The objects illustrated in this chapter are small and made of bronze, unless otherwise indicated. They are grouped by forms: horses, bulls, etc. Datings are approximate.

52
Plaque: Figures with Cart Drawn by Mules
Siberian or Ordos, 7th century (?) B.C.
Arthur Sackler Collection, New York

53
Pin: Crouching Horse
Luristan, 10th or 9th century B.C.
Indiana University Art Museum

54
Shaft Terminal: Crouching Horse
Ordos, 7th century B.C.
Heeramaneck Collection

55
Buckle: Horse
6th-5th century B.C.
Indiana University Art Museum

Similar pieces have been found in Ordos, China, Korea, and Japan.

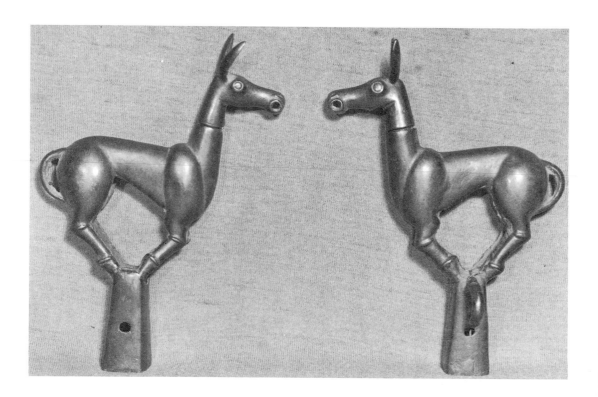

Pole Ends: Standing Horses
Ordos, 7th century B.C.
Heeramaneck Collection

Khingan) range on the west and the Hsiao Khingan (Little Khingan) range on the east. These boundaries define the Nonni watershed, which is Manchuria proper.

Both Djungaria, that portion of East Turkestan which lies north of the T'ien Shan and west of the Altai and Mongolia, and Mongolia are compartmented regions. Djungaria south of the Irtysh is an excellent area for the pastoral way of life, and often served as a nuclear region of an important nomadic tribal confederation. But the great mountain barriers prevent indefinite expansion and also impede political unity. Similarly, Mongolian steppe dwellers could not expand beyond the mountains to the west, north, and east, and to the south, where the steppe blends into the North China plain, expansion was effectively blocked by the great sedentary civilization of China. For the greater part of its history, China was governed by a unified and well ordered administration which had powerful military forces at its disposal.

The prevailing pastoral way of life in much of the Eurasian steppe suggests the nature of the archaeological material to be found in the region. Though agriculture never disappeared after the emergence of pastoralism, the herding chieftains constituted a warrior ruling class possessing the greater part of the accumulated wealth, except in Khorezm where irrigation agriculture had prospered since early times. Affluence and status were expressed through personal adornment, military gear, and horse trappings, articles which were particularly suited to the animal style of decor, and through which the style found its most vivid and varied expression. Although the extensive spread of the

57

Bull

Central Europe, Hallstatt period, 1000 B.C. or earlier
Heeramaneck Collection

58

Man Astride a Bull

Possibly Sardinian, 10th century B.C.
Burton H. Berry Loan Collection, Indiana University

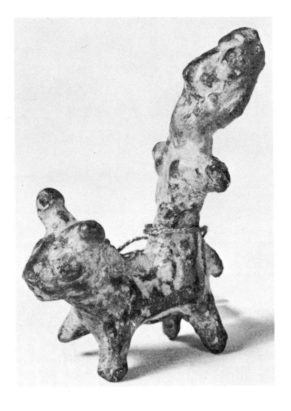

59

Bull

Possibly from Crete, first millennium B.C.
Burton H. Berry Loan Collection, Indiana University

Eurasian animal style is certainly associated with the growth of Scythian power, the origins of this unique style remain obscure and a survey of the early history of the region may provide some useful clues.

Since the Second World War Soviet archaeological investigators, who now have a virtual monopoly in the greater part of the region, have come upon material which completely changed our picture of cultural development on the Eurasian steppe in ancient times. The most striking feature of these discoveries is their uniformity over the region for relatively long periods since the Middle Bronze phase.

The problem of reconstructing the pre- and proto-history of Eurasia on the basis of archaeological material, supplemented by the relevant fragments of literary references from peripheral regions of high culture, differs considerably from that encountered in the Ancient Near East or even China. The most significant difference is the general lack of stratigraphic evidence in Eurasia, where, as a rule and over fairly extensive regions, a site contains but one cultural level and an area but one culture phase. The lack of good stratigraphic evidence is largely due to the vastness of the territory and the nomadic way of life of its inhabitants. Thus a relative chronology based on typology is the best available. Instances in which Eurasian material closely corresponds with that from high culture regions with fairly well established chronologies make possible a closer determination of the chronological limits of the Eurasian material.

One such region is Minussinsk in south Siberia. The Minussinskii Krai, located on the upper Yenisei just north of the Zapadnii Sayan range, has five rather well defined sequences dating from Early Bronze, about late third millennium, to the early centuries of our era. The culture sequences in the Minussinsk region are designated as follows: Afanasievo, third to early second millennium B.C.; Andronovo, ca. 1700 to 1200 B.C.; Karasuk, 1200 to 700 B.C.; Tagar, 700 to late first millennium B.C.; Hunno-Sarmatian, late first millennium B.C. to early centuries of our era. These dates approximate those suggested by Kiselev. In each case important similarities with other cultures, some at considerable distances, are noteworthy.

According to Kiselev, the Afanasievo sphere extended from the upper Yenisei to the upper Irtysh. Sites containing typical burials of the Afanasievo complex are to be found in this region. Specific elements, however, have affinities with similar elements elsewhere. For example, Afanasievo clay vessels and rattles resemble those of southeastern European Russia. Some Western affinities extend back into pre-Afanasievo times; the pre-Afanasievo ceramics of the Altai resemble those of the Kelteminar culture of Khorezm. In passing it may be noted that neither Afanasievo nor pre-Afanasievo skulls show any Mongoloid characteristics. The mixed economy of the Afanasievo people is typical of the Eurasian steppe in ancient times. They raised domestic animals, including horned cattle, sheep, and horses and supplemented their food supply by hunting, and to a limited extent, agriculture. If the Afanasievo finds contain the bones of domesticated horses dating from the early third millennium, the horse must have been known to the Afanasievo people before its appearance in the Ancient Near East.

60
Bull with Ring in Nose
Possibly from Western Asia, date undetermined
Indiana University Art Museum

Cultural Diffusion from An-Yang to the Danube / 55

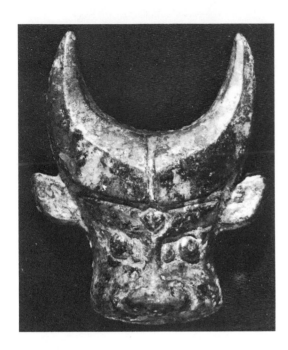

61
T'ao t'ieh Mask, in the form of a buffalo's head
Chinese, Shang dynasty
Indiana University Art Museum

62
Buckle with Crouching Buffalo at One End and
Bird at the Other
Chinese, Chou period
Indiana University Art Museum

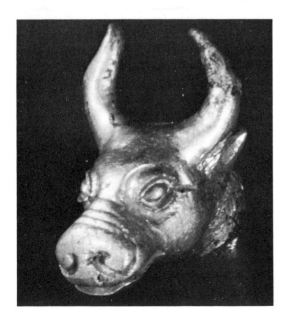

63
Head of Buffalo
Probably Chinese of the Han period (gold)
Indiana University Art Museum

According to Debets, the old Europoid of Siberia must have made contact with the old Mongoloid of East Asia along the Yenisei. The old Europoids of the Afanasievo culture were the earliest cattle herders of south Siberia. In the second millennium they began to raise large herds of sheep and their influence spread both north and east where they were in contact with Neolithic hunting and fishing folk. The Afanasievo sphere extended to the Baikal region where it impinged on the Glazkovskii culture, presumably that of a Tungusic folk. These contacts continued into the Andronovo period. The white jade of the South Baikal region, which provided much material for the tools and ornaments of the Glazkovskii folk, was the source of the white nephrite for the Shang Chinese.

Andronovo culture, the next phase of the Minussinsk Bronze Age, reaches over a far greater region. Characteristic Andronovo sites extend from the Minussinsk region to western Siberia, where these blend with the Srubnie culture of South and East Russia and the Seima-Turbino culture of Northeast Russia. The region of overlap with the Srubnie culture extends eastward from the Ural River to the shores of the Aral Sea, and to the south beyond Khorezm in the Syr Darya and Amu Darya region.

Andronovo is a full Bronze Age culture. The universal use of wool and hides of domestic animals indicates an expanding herding economy. The physical type of the Andronovo people suggests no change from their apparent direct descendents, the bearers of the Afanasievo culture, a basic type which persists well into the Tagar period. Kiselev is inclined toward the view that there is continuity from one to the other and that these are somehow related to the Kelteminar culture of Khorezm.

While many features of the next phase of the Minussinsk Bronze Age culture, Karasuk, indicate a continuity with the preceding Andronovo, others point to a foreign intrusion. In the West, Andronovo is not succeeded by a Karasuk phase but gradually develops into a Tagar culture. There are similar Andronovo survivals on the northeastern fringes of the Andronovo sphere where it impinges on the Glazkovskii region. Karasuk thus appears as a wedge driven into the Andronovo sphere.

The principal new elements in Karasuk culture are a considerable increase in the quantity of bronze weapons and tools including the crescent-shaped knife with loop or animal-head terminals on the grip, the fashioning of the straight dagger with hollow handle, and the development of some skeletal variations indicating an infusion of Mongoloid somatic type. These characteristics are accompanied by indications of a significant increase in population density, an increase in the number of sheep with a corresponding decrease in the relative number of cattle and horses, and the virtual absence of game animals. The Karasuk people seem to have eaten much less meat than their predecessors and could not have been hunters. The Mongoloid infusion, the Shang form of the Karasuk knife, and the presence of agriculturalists and shepherds all point to affinity with the Chinese culture sphere, particularly that of the Shang people at Anyang.

Kiselev provides a concise summary of the arguments for the Chinese

64
Stag
Possibly Hittite, before 1500 B.C.
Burton H. Berry Loan Collection, Indiana University

65
Affronted Ibexes
Luristan, 10th century B.C.
Indiana University Art Museum

66
Cheekpiece: Ibex
Luristan, 10th century B.C.
Indiana University Art Museum

67
Standing Ibex
Possibly Anatolian, 10th century B.C.
Burton H. Berry Loan Collection

68
Square Plaque: Stag and Other Animals
From the Caucasus, 5th century or later (silver)
Heeramaneck Collection

69
Stag
Siberian, 7th century B.C.
Indiana University Art Museum

70
Doe
Ordos, 7th century B.C. or later
Indiana University Art Museum

71
Plaque: Three Cervids
Ordos, 7th century B.C.
Arthur Sackler Collection

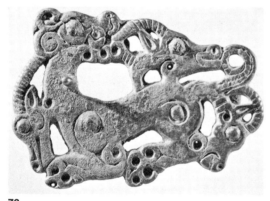

72
Plaque with Three Ibexes
Siberia or Ordos, 7th century B.C.
Arthur Sackler Collection

origin of Karasuk culture. Its close affinity with the culture of the Ordos region of Suiyuan Province suggests a spread of Karasuk culture from southeast to northwest into the Minussinsk region, with traces as far as Karaganda in the Kazakh steppe. This description agrees with Karlgren's contention that the early Siberian animal-style, as represented in the Karasuk phase of Minussinsk, follows rather than precedes the Shang. Kargren's chronology for Karasuk is generally in accord with that of Kiselev.

In the Minussinsk region Karasuk is followed by a culture designated as "Minussinsk Kurgan culture" by Teploukhov, who first attempted its classification. Kiselev renamed this culture Tagar, which is the term now generally employed. Like Andronovo, Tagar culture (ca. 700 to 300 B.C.) has a very wide extension. While, as a later culture, Tagar is far more complex in both internal ramification and local variations that often show different affinities, it possesses sufficient unity to justify an over-all designation. Tagar appears in three rather distinct phases, which are apparent over the greater part of the region of its extension. The first phase, Tagar I, is a Middle Bronze culture following directly on Karasuk in the Altai-Yenisei region and on Late Andronovo elsewhere. Tagar II, a Late Bronze culture, has much in common with "Early Scythian." Tagar III is an Iron Age culture with many "Late Scythian" features.

The most complete Tagar sequence is found in the Altai-Yenisei region, and this fact suggests, but does not confirm, that Altai-Yenisei was the nuclear region of Tagar culture. The question must remain

73
Shaft Terminal: Head of Ibex
Ordos, 7th-6th century
Heeramaneck Collection

74
Buckle: Contorted Cervid
Chinese, Chou period or later
Indiana University Art Museum

75
Head of Doe
Probably Chinese of the Han period (gold)
Indiana University Art Museum

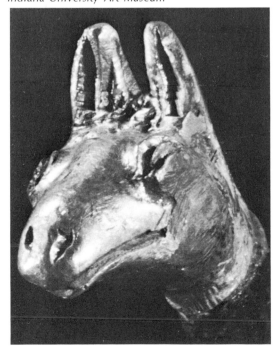

Cultural Diffusion from An-Yang to the Danube / 61

76
Tiger
Ordos, 6th century B.C.
Indiana University Art Museum

78
Plaque: Tiger Preying on Another Animal
Siberia or Ordos, 8th century B.C.
Heeramaneck Collection

77
Affronted Felines
Luristan, 10th century B.C.
Indiana University Art Collection

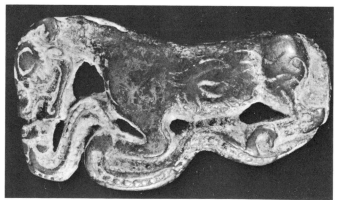

79
Tiger and Serpent
Ordos or Chinese, 6th century B.C. or later
Indiana University Art Museum

80
Cheekpiece: Archer on Chariot Drawn by a
Fantastic Animal
Luristan, 8th century B.C.
Heeramaneck Collection

81
Bird
Luristan or Han China, date undetermined
Indiana University Art Museum

83
Wild Pig
Ordos or Han Chinese, 5th century B.C. or later
Indiana University Art Museum

82
Animal With Four Heads
Ordos, 7th century B.C.
Arthur Sackler Collection

84
Squatting Bear
Chinese, Han period
Indiana University Art Museum

85
Plaque: Mastodon
Ordos, 7th or 6th century B. C.
Indiana University Art Museum

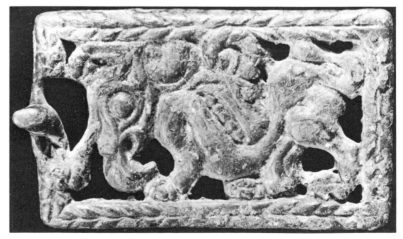

open for the time being. New features emerging in the course of Tagar development, though they appear in the same general sequence with due regard for local variations, do not seem to move in the same direction. Some appear earlier in the East, others in the West. This possible oscillation of influences from one end of the region to the other implies that there may have been much more intimate contact between East and West through the Eurasian steppe at that time than we suspected.

The problem of Tagar affinities is complex, and we shall consider only a few of the most important examples. Bronze picks of Tagar I from the Altai-Yenisei region resemble an example from the earliest Ananino burial in the Volga-Kama region dating from the sixth century B.C. and suggest diffusion from East to West. On the other hand, some Tagar composite picks contain iron blades, and a few, iron butts. These antedate the use of iron in China. Many of these composite weapons can be linked with Luristan and Mazanderan types. Bronze arrowheads of Tagar II resemble those from Scythian burials of the seventh to the fifth centuries B.C., also suggesting an East-West diffusion. The arrival of Scythians in Asia Minor and the appearance of Scythian elements in Tagar II at about the same time is probably no coincidence. However, Tagar arrowheads occur in greater variety than Scythian. The most common overlap types are variations of the triangular trefoil with a shafthole. Tagar standards from the Altai-Yenisei region resemble those from North China and Perm (Ananino). Such standards are also Caucasian and Luristan forms which antedate the Tagar forms.

86
Five Daggers
From Siberian or Ordos tomb sites, 8th to 5th centuries B.C.
Arthur Sackler Collection

The second dagger from the left is of the Karasuk type; all the others are Tagar.

87
Dagger with Ibex on Pummel and in Relief
Ordos, Tagar type, ca. 7th century B.C.
Arthur Sackler Collection

Tagar daggers with straight tapering blades developed from similar forms with hollow handles found in Karasuk burials but appear in greater quantity and variety. The Tagar dagger in some of its versions is definitely related to the *akinakes* of Scythia and Iran. The pommel of the Tagar dagger may have the following terminals: button shape, often in the form of a "Rolltier" in low relief; standing animal; and antennae terminals resembling those of some Hallstatt swords. Some iron daggers of *akinakes* type from the North Caucasus in the Scythian period (Nestorovskii) have similar antennae terminals. Pointed metal ends for the grips of battle-picks are also common. Such metal terminals are also to be found on the shafts of the Shang and Chou *ko*. The *ko*, a characteristic Chinese weapon from Shang time, is a dagger-axe used in the same manner as the Tagar battle-pick or halberd, which it antedates by at least half a millennium.

The ethnic background of the bearers of Tagar culture seems to be extremely complex. The crystallization of artifact types took place in more than one area. There is no apparent "Urheimat," and some forms first developed and widely used in the East spread to the West, while others reversed the pattern. The course of development of the Tagar cultures is somehow associated with the rise and spread of Kimmerian power and its final overthrow, at least in many regions, by the Scythians. There is evidence that many islands of Kimmerian resistance remained, which later reasserted themselves under other names. The period comes to a close with the advent of other migrations, evidently caused by the Macedonian conquest.

Soviet writers refer to the post-Tagar period as Hunno-Sarmatian and include the Pazyryk period in the Altai. The earliest references to the Sarmatians date from the late fourth century. With all deference to Rostovtzev, I am nevertheless inclined toward the view that the Sarmatians to whom the writers of the Hellenistic and Roman periods refer were the Sauromatai of the early Ionian geographers. The different cultural features of the Sarmatians vis-à-vis the Sauromatai can be accounted for by developments in the intervening period of dynamic change. The Sarmatian complex at that time included the Massagetai of the Oxus-Jaxartes region, where Alexander was forced to wage a long and bitter war. He finally succeeded, by conquest and compromise, in gaining the support of a good portion of the East Iranian nobility, who then accepted him as the legitimate successor of the Achaemenids. One can trace the orientalization of Alexander from this time.

Apparently not all the East Iranian lords of the old Massagetai complex were content to submit to Macedonian rule. Some moved west to South Russia to overthrow the now weakened Scythian kingdom. Others went east, beyond the Altai and the T'ien Shan to the northwestern borderlines of China, and there became overlords of a population which most likely was of Issedon (Kimmerian?) origin. This sketch of Sarmatian migration and expansion follows in most features that proposed by Tolstov, who led the archaeological expedition which operated in the old territory of the Massagetai. The migration explains the presence of Sarmatian culture elements in South Russia,

88
Dagger with Head of Cervid on Pummel

Chinese, Shang dynasty
Heeramaneck Collection

89
Dagger with Animal with Button-top Horns
on Pummel

Chinese, Shang dynasty
Heeramaneck Collection

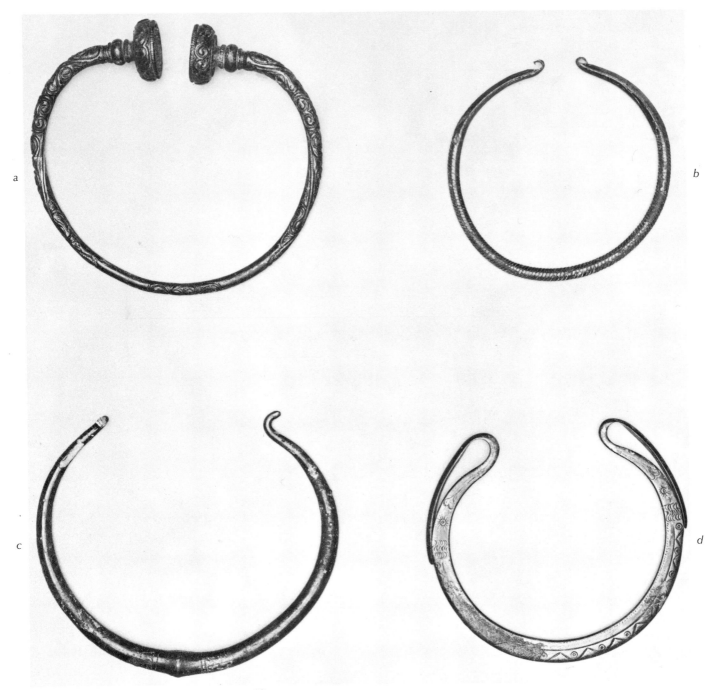

90
Four Torques

a) Celtic; b), c) Northwest Iranian; d) Scandinavian,
1st millennium B.C.
Heeramaneck Collection

the Altai, the Kansu-Ordos region, and Mongolia at that time.

Though I am inclined to regard Western Asia and the Aegean as the ultimate source of the animal-style, it is evident that the particular form of the animal-style once called Scythian and later Eurasian was brought to the West by the Scythians. This is particularly true in Hungary. The elements of the animal-style found in Hallstatt and Celtic culture probably had other sources of inspiration, but Scythian influence is not to be discounted. The animal-style elements found in Hallstatt (Late Urnfield would be a better term) culture of Europe reveal both Balkan and Inner Asian elements. Nevertheless the forms are highly stylized, petrified, utterly lacking in the tense vigor and violent movement of the Inner Asian style. Elements of the Celtic culture of the European Iron Age point to Scythia on the one hand and the Aegean on the other. The Celts were warrior merchant-adventurers whose power was based on the monopoly of weapons production and long-range trade controlled by the possession of hill forts located at strategic points, and their wide contacts made them subject to a variety of influences.

The animal-style of the West, which received a powerful impetus as a result of the rise of the European Huns at the beginning of the great Völkerwanderrung, the so-called Ars Barbarica, has clear Inner Asian affinities. The Huns themselves, however, remain will-o'the-wisp. Such new elements of material culture as can definitely be attributed to the Hunnic period appear to be of Pontic origin, and their bearers the Sarmatian people known to the Romans as the Alani. The whole problem of the origin of the European Huns remains an open question.

FOR FURTHER READING

G. Borovka, *Scythian Art*, 1928.

B. Karlgren, "Some Weapons and Tools of the Yin Dynasty," *Bulletin of the Museum of Far Eastern Antiquities*, 17, (1945).

E. H. Minns, *Scythians and Greeks*, 1913.

T. T. Rice, *The Scythians*, 1957.

M. I. Rostovtzeff, *Iranians and Greeks in South Russia*, 1922.

————, *The Animal Style in South Russia and China*, 1929.

A. Salmony, *Sino-Siberian Art in the Collection of C. T. Loo*, 1933.

Also numerous articles in French and English in the *Bulletin of the Museum of Far Eastern Antiquities*, Stockholm.

Most, if not all, of the Russian authors cited have not been translated into English. The interested student is referred to A. L. Mongait, *Archaeological Research in the U. S. S. R.*, 1961.

IV

JANE GASTON MAHLER:

The Art of the Silk Route

BY THE TIME THE T'ANG DYNASTY WAS FIRMLY ESTABLISHED, CH'ANG-AN, ITS WESTERN CAPITAL, HAD STOOD FOR AT LEAST SIX CENTURIES AS THE TERMINUS OF THE TWO GREAT ROADS that linked it to India, Persia, and the Mediterranean ports. The city was the destination of people as diverse in dress as nomads from the Mongolian steppes in their long leather coats and high boots, and the courtiers from the tropical kingdoms of Southeast Asia in gay sarongs.

In 742 A.D., Ch'ang-an's population of 1,960,188 lived in a walled rectangle about five by six miles in extent. The gates were closed at sundown, and a stir of activity came again at daybreak, when officers of the Emperor's household, with servants, purveyors, and domestics of the nobility, some on foot and some on horseback, came into the public markets to make their daily purchases.

The capital (near modern Sian-fu) had been laid out with a broad boulevard in exact center, running on the north-south axis and leading northward to an inner protected precinct that contained the Imperial Palace, which faced south. As a result the Son of Heaven and the Imperial Household were, literally, at the head (north), and thus their benign influence flowed out to the rest of the populace. Avenues and streets on a grid plan conformed to ancient tradition based on Chinese ritual needs and customs. (The same plan was carried farther east to Japan when the old city of Nara was laid out, and again when Heian-Kyo (modern Kyoto) was created in the eighth century A.D.)

The markets were situated east and west of the grand boulevard, like shoulders supporting the head. East and West, Right and Left, had particular significance in the etiquette of the court, and in prestige among the ranks of civil and military officials. Merchants lived in the western sector, with commoners. Hundreds of warehouses lined the outer wall of the great market district. Shops dealing in the same goods, and people engaged in the preparation of similar articles, or practicing the same crafts, were grouped together.

Foreigners and imported goods played a vital role in the life of Ch'ang-an, but to the Chinese they all came from the *Hu,* "Barbarian," countries. Incoming gifts were referred to as "tribute," and visiting princes were regarded as vassals by the Son of Heaven. The local literati were secure in their superiority to the outlanders; once this position was understood, newcomers were welcome in their city of diversity. Whatever strange languages were spoken, there would be someone who could translate, and whatever odd dietary requirements had to be met, the viands could be found. Those who longed to hear exotic music, or to buy colorful garments were happily satisfied.

About 631, 3,260 students, largely Chinese, were enrolled in the National Academy, but as young men came from Korea, Japan, and Central Asia, the figure rose to about 8,000. In the Buddhist temple compounds monks worked at translating numerous texts that originated in India or Ceylon or Central Asia. Even before the Master of the Law, Hsüan-tsang, journeyed from China to India (628-645) to study and collect source materials, a considerable body of Buddhist literature had been translated into Chinese. The books of other faiths—Zoroastrian, Manichaean, Jewish, Christian, and Hindu—also were studied and discussed. Their adherents were permitted to build their own places of worship in Ch'ang-an.

The northern Chinese had become accustomed to having foreigners in their midst much earlier than the T'ang period; in the late Chou period traffic with the nomads, and, in Han times, the active trade with Rome had made them familiar with the ways of foreign lands. Among the products brought in were gold dust, precious stones, asbestos, tortoise shell, ivory, and horses of fine Central Asian breed. The caravans heading westward carried furs, ceramics, lacquer, silks, and bronze objects such as belthooks, weapons, and mirrors.

During Han times, when the empire included parts of Korea and Indo-China and Chinese culture had taken root in the peripheral areas, the great Chinese cities attracted migrant musicians, entertainers, craftsmen, and men learned in astronomy, medicine, and philosophy. They made their way up from Burma, or from the southern seaports, or came by caravan though the Jade Gate of Tun-huang in Kansu province.

With the collapse of central authority in the fourth century A.D., the nomads in North China became more daring, penetrating deeper into Chinese territory and finally establishing themselves as rulers in the period of the Six Dynasties. When a Chinese again became the Son of Heaven, in the Sui period, the prestige of traditional culture had not diminished in spite of the mixed population; ancient literature, rituals, and etiquette had survived during the long interval. The barbarians had been well schooled as generation succeeded generation.

In the post-Han period of disruption, Buddhism gained ground. The Northern Wei rulers were liberal patrons of the arts, responsible for the cave-temple complexes such as those at Tun-huang, Yün-kang, and Lung-mên, which are regarded as being among the greatest treasures in modern China, in spite of damage, pilferage, and crude restoration over the centuries.

The spiritual needs, both of the Chinese and nomads, found expression in an art of an ethereal quality that is all the more remarkable because it grew out of a time of uncertainty and ferment, of frustration, resentment, and arrogance. The benign grace of the Buddha ideal shines through the work of gauche newcomers and indigenous craftsmen who were moved from place to place at the whim of the ruling house.

Though the Buddha and his attendants had to be portrayed according to iconographic rules stemming from India, minor figures, attributes and details of setting were treated with considerable freedom. The Lokapala, or mythological guardians of the Four Directions in Hindu cosmology, resembled Chinese army officers; spirits of earth and sky were composites of foreign and local deities; dragons replaced cobras in the stories about Shakyamuni; the incense burner was the familiar *po shan lu,* Mountain of Taoist Immortals, transformed; monks usually were shown as foreigners with big noses and deep-set eyes. Art styles were as mixed as the polyglot population.

As a result of this continuous contact during several preceding centuries, foreign products and people were fashionable in Ch'ang-an by

95

91
Glass Beads
Chinese, Found in Old Loyang, 5th century B.C.
Royal Ontario Museum, Toronto

92
Bronze Plaque with Revolving "Eyes"
Chinese, Chou dynasty, 5th-3d century B.C.
Royal Ontario Museum

Chinese glass found in Chou dynasty sites contains lead and barium. Glass which contains neither is presumed to have come from Egypt.

93
Ivory Combs with Bird Ornament
Chinese, T'ang dynasty
Arthur Sackler Collection

94
Fragment of Draw-loom Silk
Found at Dura Europos
Yale University Art Gallery

If this piece of woven silk is Chinese it presumably dates from the third or second century B.C. (or later) and thus represents the principal commodity which gave its name to the Silk Route. If the piece was made in Syria, silk thread must have been imported from China unless sericulture was known in the Near East at an early epoch.

the eighth century. Ladies used cosmetics brought in from Persia; they rode astride and played polo like Tibetans. The whirling dancers from Central Asia outshone the dignified girls who entertained the court with the gentle sleeve-dance, and imported horses were trained to perform to music. Horses of sturdier breed, trained for cavalry campaigns, took the Chinese army across deserts and mountains far to the west, often under the command of non-Chinese officers.

The change from customary dress to new fads, and the acceptance of strangers as a normal part of the passing scene, is most vividly recorded in the form of *ming ch'i*, or tomb figurines. These are not mournful mementos; rather, they are gay and charming miniature sculptures in clay. Ranging in height from a few inches to nearly life-size, glazed or unglazed depending on the rank of the deceased person, the figures were placed on the floor of the tomb chamber, around the coffin. Guardians stood near the door to frighten intruders. Then came camels and horses and carts, and finally members of the household, or entertainers, to make the spirit feel at home.

In recent years *ming ch'i* have been unearthed by the thousands. Among the West Asians modelled by Chinese potters, we can recognize Persians, Armenians, Jews, Khorezmians, Turks, Khotanese and other inhabitants of the oasis-cities, and, from Southeast Asia, Annamese or a neighboring tropical type whose sarong seems inadequate for life in North China. Each figurine is designed to show the person in his or her characteristic dress, from which, in most instances, we can identify the occupation. There are merchants and peddlers, caravan men, grooms, soldiers, falconers, wine sellers, dancers, musicians, scribes, civil officials, and courtiers. Relatives and servants, dogs and other pets, and miniature utensils were also part of the menage in the sepulcher.

95

Lokapala or Guardian Divinity
Chinese, 5th century or later (polychrome clay)
Indiana University Art Museum

96

Patera: Jupiter and Ganymede (?)
From Taxila, 1st to 3d century (steatite)
William Rockhill Nelson Gallery of Art

The wish for realism in sculpture is, in itself, a reflection of Western influence. Chinese art of pre-Han and Han times had been concerned with capturing the essence, the inner vitality, rather than the externals of form. Superfluous details were discarded; the imagination of the observer was challenged by every subtle nuance of line. The unsaid was as important as the spoken word, the vacuum was essential for a vortex.

Across the world, the literal-minded Romans preferred portraiture and descriptive art—and most of the people of the Mediterranean basin were part of the Roman empire. This wave of realism surged eastward. The Parthians who controlled Iran, the Kushans to the east of them, and the parts of India under Kushan sovereignty produced images of themselves that were true to life. In the stucco and terra-cotta figurines of places such as Taxila and Hadda in old Gandhara, we see accurate reflections of the ethnic strains who traded together, or lived and worshipped together there. They are depicted in all of their variety of feature, of age, and mood. This movement of realism reached China in the period of the Six Dynasties, and gained momentum until its climax in the T'ang period.

The mythology of the Greco-Roman world had penetrated Gandhara and the Ganges Valley at the time that Buddhist iconography was in a

97
Patera: Figure Riding a Serpent
From Taxila, 1st to 3d century (steatite)
Eilenberg Collection, New York

98
Patera: Angel Astride a Dragon
From Taxila, 1st to 3d century (steatite)
Eilenberg Collection

99
Reliquary Lid with Floral Design
From Gandhara, 3d-5th century
Eilenberg Collection

formative stage. Tritons, Herculean weight-bearers, cherubs dancing **112** among laurel garlands of victory, angels, Bacchanalian revellers, guardian deities of cities, the gods of Olympus and Baalbek entered **96** into Buddhistic religious and secular art.

As Buddhism spread, the arts in the lands of the new converts, especially in communities bordering the southern trade route, were affected by Mediterranean innovations. In the ruins of Yarkand, Khotan, Dandanuiliq, Niya, and Miran, bits of architectural ornament, moldings and panels, cabinet work and murals clearly reflect the diffusion of motifs from the West, and from India. The famous angels of Miran, painted by Tita (Titus) in the third century A.D., with their large, elo- **115** quent eyes and feather-wings, could have come from a Roman wall. **116** Men in Scythian-Phrygian caps might have come from Anatolia to pay their respects to the Buddha, and ladies looking like Coptic beauties seem to gaze in unabashed awe at the Buddha's disciples with their shaven heads.

In Afghanistan, most of the caravans halted at checkpoints, such as Kapisça (modern Begram). Many of the products of transcontinental trade remained there, buried as disaster came to the city, to be discovered by archaeologists of the twentieth century. Chinese lacquer and Syrian glass have been found by excavators, and carvings in ivory and bone, too fragile to have survived in their tropical homeland, India. The combs, boxes, plaques, and ornamental panels of the sec- **93** ond or third centuries A.D. that survived in the Afghan soil, preserved the elegance and sensual grace of the artistic style of North India as truly as did the monumental sculpture of the Buddhist stupa at Sanchi. One of the ladies carved in ivory was discovered in Italy, in the ruins of Pompeii, while other ivory pieces inspired imitators in China.

Portable objects such as these, light in weight and reasonably durable, are the bearers of authentic art motifs from one region to another. Whereas a sketch or model of a famous image rarely retains the style of the original, the ivories, the textiles, small metalcrafts, manuscripts, and ceramics, once they arrive at their destination, can be handled by the local craftsmen. They can be kept in the shop or in the home, unlike the solemn ritual images, and may exert a direct influence for centuries thereafter.

As India and Iran, long the cultural and intellectual leaders of Asia, grew weak, the center of power shifted to China in the T'ang era. Enriched by the mid-Eastern cultures, Chinese art and thought attained a splendor that became proverbial. In religious literature and art India had played the major role, but in the secular fields of fashion, textile design, metalwork, and pottery, Sasanian Persia effected a profound change in Chinese designs and techniques, from the sixth century through the eighth. For instance, in rock-cut reliefs of the investiture of Sasanian kings, a circlet of pearls with floating ribbons—a part of royal regalia in this solemn ritual—was bestowed upon the King of Kings by Ahuramazda, the god of Light. When adapted to fabrics or stucco ornaments on the palaces, or used on silver plates and pitchers, the circlet contained the si-murg (a composite fabulous creature, part bird and part beast), a cock, or a boar's head (a gift brought to the

King at the New Year's festival), or a tree of life, or foliate patterns. All of the symbols suggest renewal of life, or regal power. Among the fragments of Sasanian fabric found along the northern silk route, and in the hidden library in the Caves of the Thousand Buddhas near Tunhuang, Chinese adaptations of these designs were found also. In Japan, the easternmost repository, textiles in Persian style were laid away in **157** the Shosoin collection in the mid-eighth century, or kept in other temple treasuries.

119 The circlet of pearls also appears in frescoes along the northern road, and on small articles such as the lid of a lacquer box. Seven pearls surrounding a single one, also a Sasanian motif, is seen as a beauty mark on the faces of fashionable ladies, and in ceramic design. The pearl medallion was incorporated in Chinese sculpture as early as the Northern Ch'i period.

The acceptance of foreign motifs, shapes, and colors induced a subtle change in Chinese aesthetics. The dynamics of such traditional themes as the dragon among clouds had evolved from Taoist theories of the two energies, the *yang* (masculine, positive) and *yin* (feminine, negative), in a state of flux—an interaction of forces best expressed in unbalanced composition of filled and vacant areas. With the influx of Persian goods came the different conception of symmetrical, or contained, components arranged in a radical design, or of an axis flanked by equal elements.

The new fashion from Iran affected the traditional significance and pattern of the Chinese bronze mirrors. During the late Chou and Han periods the mirrors were intended for use in Taoist ceremonies and were of cosmic significance. The design represented in microcosm the order of Heaven, the flow of magnetic forces, of clouds and winds, of one season following close upon another. Part of the design was precisely calculated, part of it fluid, linear, imaginative. But Iranian foliate designs and roundels began to replace the Four Quadrant Animals, the Queen Mother who regulated the Western region, and the King who regulated the East. Grapes and lions, both of exotic West Asian origin, were popular in T'ang times until a proscription against foreign religions (such as Buddhism) and the foreigners who practiced them, was proclaimed in 845 A.D., by which time the mirrors were no longer cast.

Early T'ang art focused on the beauties of the material world rather than upon the mysteries of heaven. Butterflies, seasonal flowers, pairs of birds, and pairs of other creatures were assembled as marriage symbols on mirrors used by brides when being taken in a palanquin to the home of the groom for the ceremony. Other metal arts reflect **146** the change in form and style. Lobed oval bowls, stem cups, long-**151** necked pitchers, and plates with regular, radial segments of ornament were obviously inspired by Iran. In pottery the same trends affected shape and design.

A basic conflict between Indian and Persian ideas in mural painting came to be resolved in Central Asia. From prehistoric times, the Indian artist had been concerned with states of consciousness, states of emotion, the breath of life, and form that was endowed with energy; in

100
Lady Musician
Chinese, Sui period (tomb figurine in green glazed pottery)
The Metropolitan Museum of Art, Rogers Fund, 1923

101
Palmyran Lady
2nd to 4th century (stone tomb relief)
Indiana University Art Museum

102
Astarte
From North Syria, 5th century (bronze statuette)
William Rockhill Nelson Gallery

103
A Caucasian Disciple of Buddha
From Hadda, 3d to 5th century (stucco head)
Seattle Art Museum, Eugene Fuller Memorial
Collection

sculpture he was most successful in giving expression to the inner life where his preference for volume and three-dimensional solidity found a proper outlet. He thought of his sculpture in relation to the changing light—either of the out-of-doors where drifting clouds hid the sun, or of the temple where flickering devotional lamps would reveal a figure for a moment, then leave it in darkness—which was part of his normal experience. The Indian artist carried this concern with volume and depth over into painting. In the Buddhist frescoes in the Ajanta cave-temples, highlights and graded tones, rather than shadows cast from a single source of light are used. Man should be in his natural setting, for man and his environment were inseparable. Each contains a portion of Universal energy.

In Persia, the emphasis had been on decorative value rather than on an expression of universal truth. The artists worked to isolate form, stylize musculature of animals, and create patterns of clear color in glazed brick on surfaces deliberately kept flat.

Where Persia was strong politically and culturally—in old Bactria, in Ferghana and Sogdiana, notably in the Pyanjikent murals, and in settlements in the Tarim River basin—Sasanian aesthetic ideas prevailed. Volume is replaced by stylization: a circle denotes a kneecap, overlapping planes indicate spatial recession, and graded tones become flat colors, with lapis lazuli blue, earthen browns, and green used in an arbitrary way. The designation of this second major art period in Central Asia as the Blue-Green period distinguishes it from the first phase of the southen silk road, which was Romano-Mediterranean in charac-

104

Head of an Occidental Man

Chinese, T'ang dynasty (glazed earthenware)
Seattle Art Museum, Eugene Fuller Memorial
Collection

105

Armenoid Wine Merchant

Chinese, T'ang dynasty (glazed earthenware)
Seattle Art Museum, Eugene Fuller Memorial
Collection

ter. In both phases, however, the subject matter was primarily Indian, conventions of iconography were drawn from India, and evidences of Indian style persist through the centuries. This process of assimilation and transformation in the arts may perhaps be better understood through a brief examination of the important centers along the silk route.

Hephthalites, Turks, and Iranians lived in Samarkand in the sixth century. Both Buddhism and Mithraism were honored. People there delighted in drinking wine, dancing, and engaging in commerce. In the seventh century Ferghana and Sogdiana had close diplomatic ties with China: their rulers were given diplomas of investiture by the Emperor, and gifts including carpets and dancing girls, and the fine breed of Ferghana horse called "the Horse of Heaven" were exchanged. In 744 bonds were cemented more firmly when an Imperial Chinese princess was given as wife to the King.

By the mid-eighth century, Islam had penetrated beyond the eastern border of Iran. A Chinese expeditionary force met and was defeated by the Arabs and their allies at Talas in 751 A.D. Among the prisoners taken by the Muslims were Chinese craftsmen, some of whom remained in Samarkand where they taught the local people to make paper. By the end of the tenth century paper had replaced papyrus and parchment in all of the Islamic countries to the west, and one of the most valuable arts had passed to the Near East and Europe from China.

Merchandise in the bazaars included, as W. Barthold informs us, "soft fabrics, copper lamps, Tabari tissues, grease, sheepskins, oil for anoint-

106

Semitic Merchant

China, T'ang dynasty (glazed earthenware)
Royal Ontario Museum

107

Khorezmian Merchant

Chinese, Sui dynasty (glazed earthenware)
Royal Ontario Museum

108

Kashgar Peddler

Chinese, T'ang dynasty (polychrome earthenware)
Seattle Art Museum, Eugene Fuller Memorial
Collection

107

108

106

ing the head, . . . sables, miniver, ermines, fur of steppe foxes, martens, beavers, . . . wax, arrows, birch bark, high fur caps, fish glue, amber, honey, hazelnuts, falcons, swords, Slavonic slaves, . . . grapes, raisins, almond paste, sesame, Samarqandi stuffs, silver colored fabrics, large copper vessels, goblets, tents, stirrups, bridles, . . . satin exported to the Turks, silken cloth, horses and mules." Traders in the market places were surely as varied in ethnic background and appearance as the goods they brought in, or bartered for.

When the caravans headed east, a favorite stopping place was Kutcha. It was blest with good water and fertile fields of millet, wheat, and rice, orchards of pear, plum, peach, apricot, and pomegranite trees, and the vines yielded great clusters of grapes. The area was also rich in gold, copper, iron, lead, and tin.

When the Chinese monk Hsüan-tsang went to Kutcha in the seventh century, he commented on the moderate climate and the honest ways of the people. They had skill with wind and stringed instruments, could play by ear and improvise, but had developed musical notation. They loved dancing and merrymaking. It was a local custom to flatten

109
Bearded Warrior with Shield
Chinese, 6th century (polychrome earthenware)
Indiana University Art Museum

110
Chinese Warrior with Caucasian Features
Chinese, T'ang dynasty (glazed earthenware)
William Rockhill Nelson Gallery of Art

111
Uighur Turk
Chinese, T'ang dynasty (unglazed white clay)
Royal Ontario Museum

the head of the newborn with a piece of wood. Men, except for the King, wore their hair short (unlike the Turks whose long, dark hair was braided). In the frescoes they are shown as red-haired, or with wavy brown hair. They were fair-skinned, with blue eyes, small noses, and short upper lips. In many ways they resemble Celtic Europeans.

Politically the Kutchans had a long association with China, from 383 A.D. through the T'ang period. In records of the fourth century, Chinese historians described the palace of the King, which possessed the splendor of an abode of the spirits, and praised the beauty and elegance of the women. The ladies of the city used cosmetics from Iran, and wore tight-sleeved gowns with fitted bodices, usually with pleated silk at the elbow. They protected their fair skins with veils. (This custom, of course, preceded the introduction of Islam to Central Asia and had nothing to do with the Muslim requirement that a woman hide her face.) The low-cut gowns did not cover the body entirely, as in the Han-Chinese fashion, nor did feminine attire include the diaphanous scarves and heavy jewelry of the women of India. When Kutchan styles were introduced in China in the sixth century, they caused a revolution in fashion.

In 581, on the occasion of a banquet given by the Son of Heaven, orchestras were sent to China from India, Bokhara, Samarkand, Kash-

112
Garland-bearing *putti*
From Gandhara, 3d century (relief in grey schist)
Royal Ontario Museum

113
Dancer from Southeast Asia
Chinese, T'ang dynasty (polychrome earthenware)
Royal Ontario Museum

114
Bearded Acrobat
Chinese, 4th-6th century (unglazed earthenware)
William Rockhill Nelson Gallery of Art

115

Detail of a fresco from a ruined Buddhist chapel at Miran

3d-4th century
From F. H. Andrews, Wall-paintings from Ancient
Shrines in Central Asia, *1948*

116
Detail of a head from the same fresco

117
Hieratic Figure on a Bracket
From Taxila, 1st to 3d century (micaceous schist)
Eilenberg Collection

gar, the country of the Turks, Kutcha, Cambodia, and Japan. One of the Kutchan demonstration-dances was called the Five Lions, one of several masked dances taken over by the Chinese, Koreans, and Japanese. Today, in celebrating the New Year, our citizens of Chinese derivation still perform the so-called Dragon-dance, which is descended from the Kutchan Lion-dance, in American cities.

Most of the Kutchan population and the royal family were Buddhists of Hinayana (Lesser Vehicle) adherence. Travelers have described the temples, their domed ceilings, and colorful murals. The frescoes have survived to give us a picture of the people, and their pictorial arts. Painting began in the fourth century, went through several phases— first Indo-Iranian, then strongly Iranian in the sixth century, and increasingly Chinese in two of the Quintura caves of the seventh and eighth century phase. The frescoes depict a feudal society; differences in rank are shown by the type of weapon carried, or the cut and color of garment. The tailored tunics, in Persian style, made of heavy silk, and the soft, pointed boots are clearly derived from Sasanian fashions.

Kutcha was one of the pleasantest cities on the long, old road. From it routes led north into steppe country across grazing lands of the nomads of Djungaria, and south, following the bed of the Khotan river crossing the Taklamakan desert, to Khotan. This city had every advantage as a trade center—a cosmopolitan place where Persian, Indian, nomadic, and Chinese cultural streams mingled. The people, who were dispersed several times during the T'ang period when Chinese armies attacked their city to punish it for its rebellious attitude (and for holding back taxes), seem to anticipate the lords and ladies of medieval Europe, in their dress, etiquette, and love of troubadour entertainment.

The Art of the Silk Route / 81

118

118

Bust of a Human with an Elephant's Head on his Chest

Found in a ruined Buddhist chapel at Kyzil, 7th-8th century (painted stucco)
From Le Coq, Die Buddhistische Spätantike in Mittelasien (Die Plastike)

119

Detail of a Painted Reliquary

From Kutcha, 7th century
From M. Bussagli, Painting in Central Asia

Continuing toward China, the caravans would make their way to Qarashahr, then to the large oasis at Turfan. The region had originally been settled by people of the same stock as the Kutchans—the Tocharian-speaking, fair-skinned people. Later nomads mingled with them, especially eastern Turks, and Chinese had been their administrators for a long time before the T'ang period. The numerous towns include Murturq, Astana, Bezeklik, and Kotscho. By the eighth century Bezeklik and Kotscho were occupied by the Uighur Turks, who remained dominant; their descendants are still an important group in East Turkestan.

Much of the Turkish population had accepted Buddhism, but their Khans were followers of Manichaeism, and a large number of Christians lived in the region. Fragments of painting, both as miniatures in manuscripts, and murals, found in the ruins of the religious foundations of these three major groups, added greatly to our knowledge of the people and their arts.

Bits of Manichaean texts in Uighur script enclosed by brilliant borders of flowers, or scenes in which worshippers may be seen in white robes before altar tables, are unique reminders of the religion and art of Mani. Some 300 years after the martyrdom in Persia of this religious figure who was equally famous as a painter, one of his clergy converted the Khan of the Uighurs while he was residing in Ch'ang-an. The Khan and his Turkish relatives formed the core of a strong group that gave prestige to Manichaeism in Asia. The Eastern Turks kept this blend of Western and Eastern religious ideas and practices alive in Turfan.

These Turks, as portrayed in ninth-century frescoes, both Manichaean **121** and Buddhist, are distinguished by straight black hair, prominent curving noses, dark slanting eyes, and a dignified bearing. Their city, Qarakhoja, was an enormous square covering about 256 acres enclosed within stamped mud walls some 22 yards high. More than 70 towers that strengthened the wall were still standing when von Le Coq visited the old fortress. The only temples found standing were of Iranian style with dome-shaped roofs, or stupas of Indian origin. Buddhist, Christian, Manichaean, and Zoroastrian writings were discovered in manuscript form, a clear evidence of the liberal attitude of the Turkish rulers to men of all faiths.

Murals were found in Bezeklik, near Murturq, dating from the ninth and tenth centuries for the most part, the period of Uighur sovereignty. They constitute the third main phase of Central Asian painting. The favorite pigments are the five classical Chinese colors—red, blue-green, yellow, black, and white—in contrast to the Indo-Iranian frescoes of the second major art period in the Kutcha region, which were done predominantly in brown, lapis blue, and bright green. As one would expect in the oasis settlement nearest China, the character of the work differs from that in the West, especially in its strong linear vitality. The work, however, reflects Turkish taste, physiognomy, and love of bright, clear designs.

When the Ottoman Turks rose to power in Anatolia and the Sultans assembled painters to illumine the manuscripts that recalled their past

120

Various Kings Worshipping at the Feet of the
Buddha

*Bezeklik, 8th-9th century (detail of a fresco in a
ruined chapel)*
From Andrews, Wall-paintings from Ancient Shrines
in Central Asia

121

Uighur King

*Found at Chotscho, 7th-8th century (from a banner
painting)*
From Le Coq, Chotscho

history and their festivals and military campaigns, the influence of
Uighur art became discernible in the art of the sixteenth and seventeenth centuries. It is curious to note that the cultural effect of the
trade between East and West, as carried on via the Silk Route, culmi-
nated in Istanbul. To the hieratic beauty of Byzantium was added the
color of the East, and with the coming of the Venetian and the
Genoese traders in the sixteenth and seventeenth centuries, a whole
new phase of East-West relations in art was opened.

FOR FURTHER READING

W. Barthold, *Turkestan Down to the Mongol Inva-
sion,* 1928

M. Broomhall, *Islam in China,* 1910.

M. Bussagli, *Painting in Central Asia,* 1963.

R. Grousset, *De la Grèce à la Chine,* 1948.

S. Hedin, *The Silk Road,* 1938.

J. G. Mahler, *The Westerners Among the Figurines of
the T'ang Dynasty of China,* 1959.

E. Schafer, *The Golden Peaches of Samarcand,* 1963.

M. A. Stein, *Serindia,* 1912.

V DOROTHY G. SHEPHERD:

Iran Between East and West

THE UNIQUE POSITION OF IRAN IN THE CENTER OF A CONSTANTLY EXPANDING CULTURAL UNIVERSE ORDAINED HER DESTINY AS CULTURAL MIDDLEMAN BETWEEN EAST AND WEST until relatively modern times. Although the geographical center continually shifted, Iran remained firmly astride the principal routes which linked East and West until after the beginning of the sixteenth century, when the new sea route around Africa opened direct contact between the Far East and Europe.

In prehistoric times Iran stood between an East which extended no farther than the Indus Valley and the outer provinces of China and a West which for all practical purposes was bounded by the Tigris and Euphrates. By the Bronze Age, contacts with the eastern Mediterranean were well established and, judging from the evidence, extended at least indirectly as far as Anyang in northwest China. Later Greece and Rome came into focus in the West, and direct contact with India and China was established. Eventually the "West" came to mean Europe, and finally also the Western Hemisphere. It is with Iran's role as middleman in the cultural diffusion between these changing spheres of East and West that this chapter is concerned.

Even the most casual survey of the cultural exchanges between East and West reveals a staggering list of instances—both material and spiritual—in which Iran has played some part as intermediary. This role was an extremely complex one that is often difficult to follow. There was a constant interplay of influence and counterinfluence sometimes traveling back and forth over centuries. At times Iran acted only as a transmitter through which cultural elements simply passed en route from East to West or vice versa. More often such cultural elements lingered in Iran to be transformed and Iranianized before being passed on to the East or West. In many instances, Iran was the creative center from which the same cultural elements were sent out in both directions.

Most Western historians have tended to overemphasize the role of Chinese influence on the West at the expense of the total picture of East-West cultural diffusion. Although Oriental contributions to the West, particularly silk and porcelain, have been more spectacular, Western contributions to Far Eastern culture have undoubtedly been more profound and certainly began at a much earlier date. In general, the West accepted Eastern contributions in the form of actual materials or techniques, but there is little evidence, until after the firm establishment of direct East-West contact in the early seventeenth century, of an attendant cultural influence. By contrast, the West-East trade was of considerable importance in transmitting Western culture to the Far East from its very beginning in prehistoric times.

This Western emphasis is no doubt due precisely to the role of the Iranians as intermediaries. Iran served as a buffer, or a sort of filter, which kept the West from having direct contact with the East, and it was they, or their Iranian neighbors of Central Asia, who were in actual contact with the Chinese and who passed on to them those elements of Western culture which they themselves had already assimilated. As the culture of Iran was more closely allied with that of the West, the Western influences—as they reached China via Iran—were much more intact than those which traveled in the reverse direction. Iran took Chinese techniques and materials, transformed them totally, filtered out the Chinese cultural elements, and then transmitted these new Iranianized cultural forms westward. As long as Iran stood as the cultural middleman, actual exchange of East-West culture was very uneven, with the bulk of cultural influence moving eastward and the Eastern influences stopped and filtered out by Iran.

There is no evidence, for example, of Chinese religion penetrating the West, and even Buddhism got no farther than the valleys of the Oxus and the Jaxartes on Iran's eastern frontier. On the other hand, the religions of the West, particularly Christianity in its Nestorian version and Manichaeism, were widely spread throughout Central Asia and the Far East. The principal route of Buddhism was via the Iranian peoples of Central Asia; the Greco-Roman culture encountered at Gandhara was also strongly Iranianized. In the form in which it reached China, therefore, Buddhism carried along many Iranian as well as Western elements.

In the field of art, it was not until the seventeenth century, when Europe came in direct contact with China, that Eastern art had an influence on the West comparable to that which Western art had previously had on the East. For example, in spite of the great volume of Chinese silk imported into the West in Roman times, Western textiles —even the earliest silks—do not show any accompanying importation of Chinese techniques, motifs, or styles; whereas, after the silk industry became established in the West and Western silks were exported to China in the late Sasanian times, Chinese weaving techniques and textile patterns underwent an immediate revolution. The textiles that served as models for the Chinese weavers—as we will see—were those of Iran.

The scope of Iran's role in the cultural diffusion between East and West is too vast to illustrate fully here. Certain aspects will be touched upon elsewhere in this book; some have been briefly mentioned above, but others will have to be passed over in silence. For this discussion I have chosen a series of specific examples, typical of a whole host of others, within the three most important media—ceramics, metal, and textiles—which demonstrate the breadth and character of Iranian influence.

CERAMICS

The earliest evidence of Iran's role as cultural intermediary is illustrated by the painted pottery of the late Neolithic and Chalcolithic periods. The centers of the painted pottery culture of Iran, spreading like an arc from Susa to Sialk, Hissar, and Anau, formed a bridge between the painted pottery cultures of Mesopotamia and the outer regions of China at Kansu. From this time onward, there was a continuous and animated exchange between East and West in the field of the ceramic arts. A never-ending flood of materials, techniques, designs, and ideas moved back and forth across Iran.

122
Ewer
Syrian, Parthian period, 1st-2nd century (green lead glaze ware)
The Metropolitan Museum of Art, Samuel D. Lee Fund, 1941

124
Bowl, Three-color Ware
Chinese, T'ang period (ceramic)
Royal Ontario Museum

123
Amphora
Chinese, Northern Ch'i dynasty (olive green lead glaze ware)
William Rockhill Nelson Gallery of Art, Nelson Fund

It was evidently the introduction of the glass and faïence media from Egypt into China in the late Chou period which led to the first Chinese experiments with glaze. A series of identical little Egyptian blue glass beads (molded in the form of a lion), which have been found scattered, as though accidentally dropped along the trade route, in Egypt, Iran, and Honan, indicate that these materials reached China via Iran. **91**

The first direct wave of influence in the ceramic field, also from West to East, was the introduction of the green lead glazes, which had been developed in the eastern Mediterranean in the early Hellenistic period and which were especially popular in Roman times. This technique **122** was apparently not adopted at the time in Iran and it is not clear by what route it reached China, but the technique of manufacturing lead glaze was well established there in early Han times and continued in use throughout the Northern Ch'i Dynasty. The frequent assertion that **123** the green lead glaze was introduced into China via Parthian Iran cannot be proved by the existence of Iranian green glaze. For though this may have been the trade route by which these wares traveled to China, the Parthian green glaze was actually produced by quite another technique, which used an alkaline rather than the lead flux of the Greco-Roman glaze. That Parthian art did, however, also contribute to

Han ceramics, in design if not in technique, is indicated by the frequent occurrence of Western and Iranian motifs in Far Eastern art. One commonly used motif was the mounted rider executing the famous "Parthian shot" from a horse running at a "flying gallop." The "flying gallop" motif evidently originated in the Eastern Mediterranean, where we first know it in Mycenaean art, and it became a favorite theme of Parthian artists. The horses, it may be noted, are the great "blood sweating" steeds of Ferghana, in quest of which the Han emperor, Wu Ti, had sent his famous expedition to Kokand in 115 B.C.

From the beginning of the T'ang period the Chinese potters showed great initiative in experimentation. They developed considerable variety in the lead glazes they had inherited from Han; several colors were added to the palette and by adding touches of color under the glaze, which ran into it and were absorbed by it, they produced the famous **124** T'ang splashed or three-color wares. But even more important, T'ang potters began to experiment with the native materials, China clay and China stone, and succeeded in producing a totally new type of ceramic, the stonewares and porcelains, which was to bring the Chinese potters such lasting fame.

In the Near East, the coarse green alkaline glazes of the Parthian period continued to be the standard pottery type through the Sasanian period and into early Islamic times. This lack of interest in ceramic art in the Near East may have been to a degree due to the abundance and cheapness of metal with the result that metal, particularly silver, was employed for many purposes for which the Chinese—less rich in metal resources—were forced to use ceramics. The influence of Sasanian metalwork in China will be discussed later on, but the importation of Sasanian silver vessels may well have inspired the Chinese potters of T'ang to improve their wares in order to compete with these imports and with the increasing production of the silversmiths at home. The **151** extensive copying of Sasanian silver vessels by the potters would seem **153** to confirm this thesis.

128
Jar on Three Lion's Feet
Chinese, late T'ang period (blue splashed ware)
Royal Ontario Museum

129
Bowl
Iranian, Sultanabad, 14th century
(underglaze painted ware)
The Cleveland Museum of Art, Purchase from the
J. H. Wade Fund

130
Bowl
Chinese, Ming dynasty (blue and white porcelain)
The Cleveland Museum of Art, anonymous gift

It was the introduction of T'ang ceramics, both the lead glazed wares and the porcelains, in Iran and Mesopotamia in the early Abbasid period that revolutionized the ceramic industry of the Near East and, in turn, was greatly to influence the development of the ceramic arts in late medieval and renaissance Europe. Although from this time on the principal flow of influence in the ceramic field followed primarily an East-West course, there are many important instances of influences moving from West to East. In either direction, Iran was always at the focal point of these movements.

In attempting to imitate the Chinese wares, the Near Eastern potters gave up their traditional alkaline glaze and adopted the lead glaze of the Chinese three-color wares which, it is interesting to note, had now come full circle from its original home in the eastern Mediterranean. With this new technique as a point of departure, the Islamic potters embarked on an era of experimentation and creativity producing the rich repertoire of techniques and styles for which the Islamic pottery of the Middle Ages is justly famous.

The most obvious dependence on the Chinese imports is illustrated by the Near Eastern version of the three-color wares. The T'ang porcelains, particularly the creamy white ware, had the greatest influence on the Near Eastern potters. Lacking the technical knowledge and the natural resources to achieve true porcelain, they arrived at a method by which, with the addition of tin oxide to the lead glaze, they could produce an opaque, creamy white glaze, giving an effect not unlike that of white porcelain. The Islamic artists, however, with their great interest in decoration, were not content to leave their pottery plain,

125

126
127
128

but painted on it with their native cobalt, or added cobalt and turquoise in splashes. The Chinese were quick to adopt the Persian cobalt, and its use in T'ang pottery undoubtedly represents the initial step in the history of the famous blue and white wares of a later date.

It is fascinating to try to follow the many varied influences in the ceramic field as they shuttled back and forth between the East and West by way of Iran throughout the Middle Ages. The *maiolica* of Italy seems to be a far cry from the early porcelains of T'ang but, in fact, were the direct result of an attempt by the Near Eastern potters to imitate these early Chinese porcelains. It was probably at Baghdad in the ninth century that the potters learned to paint on the opaque white tin glaze with other metallic oxides. The beautiful lustre wares thus produced were, by way of the Islamic lustres of Spain and the *majolicas* of Valencia, to develop in the sixteenth and seventeenth centuries into the various tin glazed wares of the rest of Europe, known in Italy as *maiolica,* in France as *faïence,* and in England and the Low Countries as Delft. This technique was even carried to the New World by Spanish potters and established at Puebla in Mexico in the seventeenth century, where it is still practiced today.

Another technique of great consequence for both the East and West was evolved by the Iranian potters from their opaque tin glazes. This was the technique of painting in enamel colors over the glaze—the so-called *minai,* or enameled, wares of the Seljuk period and the beautiful *lajvardin* wares of the Mongol period. This technique, which represented a complete break with the Chinese tradition of monochrome porcelain, dominated the ceramic art of the Ming and Ch'ing periods. The overglaze painted wares of the Ch'ing period, particularly those of the *famille verte,* had a profound effect on the ceramic art of Europe in the eighteenth century.

Perhaps Iran's most spectacular contribution to the ceramic arts of both East and West was the use of cobalt. The precise link between
127 the early use of cobalt and white at Samarra and the blue and white porcelain of Ch'ing-te Chen in the Yüan period is not clear. It is very probable that the technique of line drawing in cobalt blue under clear glaze used in the Chinese blue and white porcelains was inspired by the late twelfth and thirteenth century blue and black underglaze painted wares of Kashan and Rakka and more directly by the derivative
129 Sultanabad wares of the Mongol period. As we have seen, the Chinese were familiar with the Iranian use of cobalt from T'ang times, and recent analyses of Chinese blue and white porcelains prove that the cobalt used was imported from Iran until the beginning of the fifteenth century, when local ore deposits seem first to have been discovered. Iran is undoubtedly the ultimate origin of this technique.

The Chinese blue and white porcelains immediately found favor in the Near East and were imported in great quantities—and evidently began to be imitated locally—before the end of the fourteenth century. They became the dominant fashion through the fifteenth century and most of the sixteenth. We know that blue and white wares were greatly prized in Iran, and the great treasure of these Chinese porcelains—many from the fourteenth century—preserved in the shrine at

131
Bowl

Turkish, Iznik, ca. 1530-40 (blue and white underglaze painted ware)
Royal Ontario Museum

132
Plate

Florentine, Medici Factory, 1575-90 (blue and white soft-paste porcelain)
The Metropolitan Museum of Art, Gift of Mrs. Joseph V. McMullan and Fletcher Fund

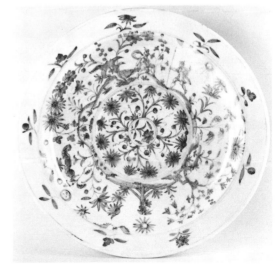

133
Bull

Mesopotamian, ca. 2500 B.C. (bronze inlaid with silver)
The Louvre Museum, Paris

134
Finial

Chinese, late Chou period, ca. 4th century B.C. (bronze inlaid with gold and silver)
The Cleveland Museum of Art, Purchase from the J. H. Wade Fund

Ardabil survives as concrete proof. In addition, Chinese ceramics predominate among the ceramics represented in the miniature paintings of the Timurid and Safavid periods. Unfortunately, however, there is little actual evidence of the manufacture of blue and white wares in Iran, though indirect evidence indicates that Tabriz may have produced such wares; the industry at Iznik is thought to have been **131** founded by potters from that city.

The beautiful blue and white soft-paste porcelains from the Medici **132** factory, which flourished briefly in Florence at the end of the sixteenth century, were a direct result of the influence of Chinese porcelains. These Chinese porcelains, however, became known in Europe by way of imports to the Near East, which reached Europe through Venetian and Genoese trade in the fifteenth and sixteenth centuries.

METAL

There seems to have been much less exchange between the East and West in the field of metalwork than in the art of other media. For lack of documents and, alas, less excusably, for lack of adequate information on the existing objects, our knowledge of the early phases of most of the metallurgical techniques is so incomplete that it is generally impossible to draw definite conclusions concerning their origins. The Bronze Age was fully developed in the Near East by about 2500 B.C. and cast bronzes have been found in all of the important Iranian sites from about that time.

Although Iran alone cannot claim credit for the westward diffusion of

Near Eastern techniques of metalworking, it did play an important role in this connection and numerous instances of direct Iranian influence can be traced. The bronze casting of ancient Greece and Etruria were certainly greatly affected by the craft as it was passed to them by way of the bronzes of Urartu. The Scythians and the Sarmatians, Iranian tribes who actually inhabited Iran for a time, were responsible to a very large extent for transmitting the techniques of metallurgy and metal smithing to the Gothic and other Germanic tribes of the Black Sea and Danube regions, from whence they were carried on into Europe. It was, of course, by these same tribes that the ancient Near Eastern animal art was carried to Europe, and to the Ordos and China.

Barnard, in his recent work on bronze casting in China, exploded for all time the myth of the Near Eastern derivation of Chinese bronze casting. However, whether the knowledge of the production of bronze, which appears in China so much later than in the Near East, was independently developed or imported is not so easily settled. At any rate, except possibly for certain weapon forms and bronze armor, particularly scale and chain mail, the Chinese bronze industry seems to have been little influenced from the West. The subsidiary technique of inlaying bronze with gold and silver may have been introduced from the Near East, where it was developed at the very beginning of the Bronze Age. We have important examples from Mesopotamia and Cappadocia dating from about 2500 B.C. and we can follow it later in Syria and in Egypt to Hellenistic and Roman times. The links illustrating its passage over Iran to China in the late Chou period are missing, but the later revival of this technique in early Islamic times in Iran led directly to its transmittal back to the West by way of the workshops of Mosul, Damascus, and Cairo to Venice in the sixteenth century. The industry at Mosul, in the heart of the Kurdish country of modern Iraq, was founded in the early thirteenth century by Iranian artisans fleeing before the advancing armies of Genghiz Khan. The name of an artist who signs himself "Mohammed al-Kurdo" on many of the Venetian inlaid metals, including the one represented here, leaves no doubt of the ultimate Iranian origin of the Venetian industry.

133
134
135
136

135
Ewer
Iranian, Seljuk period, 12th century (bronze inlaid with silver)
The Metropolitan Museum of Art

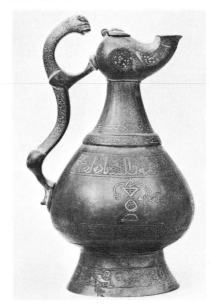

136
Salver
Venetian, 16th century (brass inlaid with silver)
The Walters Art Gallery, Baltimore

137
Pectoral
Egyptian, period of Sesostris II, 18th century B.C. (gold cloisonné)
The Metropolitan Museum of Art

138
Standing Phoenix
Chinese, T'ang period (gold cloisonné)
The Minneapolis Institute of Arts, Gift of Mrs. Stinson Pillsbury in memory of her husband

140
Bowl (detail of design)
Mesopotamian, Ortukid Prince Da'ud ibn Sukman, 1114-1144 (cloisonné enamel on copper)
Tiroler Landesmuseum Ferdinandeum, Innsbruck

139
Medallion, bust of Christ
Frankish, 8th century (cloisonné enamel on copper)
The Cleveland Museum of Art, Purchase from the J. H. Wade Fund

141
Cup Stand
Chinese, Ming dynasty (cloisonné enamel on copper)
The Metropolitan Museum of Art, Bequest of Mrs. H. O. Havemeyer, H. O. Havemeyer Collection

142
Rhyton: Kneeling Bull
Iranian, Achaemenid period (silver)
Cincinnati Art Museum

143
Rhyton Terminating in a Bull's Head, with Flying Eros Painted on Cup
Greek, Apulian, 4th century B.C. (ceramic)
The Metropolitan Museum of Art, Rogers Fund, 1903

China was much less inventive and imaginative than the Near East in working with gold and silver, perhaps to a great extent because of her less abundant resources. From the historical evidence it would seem that Chinese sources of gold were not discovered until the first century B.C. All of the gold used before that date, and evidently for a considerable time thereafter, had to be imported from great distances—probably India, Central Asia, and possibly Iran—with the result that gold was rarely used in early times. The techniques developed only very slowly and undoubtedly owed much to the Near Eastern gold- and silversmiths.

Because of her rich natural resources, and on the basis of the large number of surviving examples, priority for the early development of the techniques of goldsmithing seems to belong to Egypt. Iran very early had developed complete mastery of this art and recent discoveries at Hasanlu and Marlik reveal all the basic goldsmith techniques in full use between 1000 and 800 B.C. It is impossible properly to assess China's debt to the Near East in this field from the scanty documents available. A gold dagger hilt in the British Museum, apparently dating from the late Chou period, must have been cast by the lost wax process, as Watson has rightly observed. The use of this process, evidently still unknown to the Chinese bronze casters, would suggest that the technique came, together with the gold, from the Near East.

144
Detail of fig. 147 showing rhyton

145
Rhyton
Chinese, T'ang dynasty (ceramic)
Royal Ontario Museum

Several small cast silver vessels of about the same date in the Kempe Collection, the Fogg Museum, and others, fashioned with the characteristic Achaemenid "lobes," have generally been considered evidence of Iranian influence.

The cloisonné technique, combined with inlay of cut stones or glass paste, can be traced in Egypt to the eighteenth century B.C., the earliest known example being the pectoral of Sesostris II in the Metropolitan Museum of Art. In Iran it occurs on a dagger handle of the ninth century B.C. recently found at Hasanlu, and it was an important technique of Achaemenid times, as we know from jewelry of the Oxus treasure in the British Museum and from objects excavated at Susa in the Louvre. The cold cloisonné technique was continued in Iran in the Parthian period, from which the beautiful cloisonné of Han and T'ang were probably derived.

It is difficult to explain the delay of more than a thousand years before the appearance in China, in the late Yüan period, of cloisonné enamel, a technique which had been used in the West almost as early as cold cloisonné. The Chinese learned this technique from Iran or, in the example illustrated, the western borders of Iran. The famous cloisonné enamel bowl of the Ortukid prince of Hisn Kaifa, Da'ud ibn Sukman (1114-1144 A.D.), provides the direct link, as Garner has shown, with the cloisonné enamels of the West. This technique apparently had its origin with the Mycenaean goldsmiths around the thirteenth century B.C.; it survived in the work of the early Greek artists and eventually developed into one of the great arts of Byzantium and was widely used throughout Europe all during the Middle Ages.

The Sasanian silversmith created the greatest impact on the art of China in the T'ang period. A great deal has been written on this subject, and it has recently been thoroughly treated by Gyllensvärd in his article on T'ang silver in the *Bulletin of the Museum of Far Eastern Art*. This is one of the most striking examples in which Iran served as the creative center from which influences were sent out in both directions.

146
Fluted Bowl
Chinese, T'ang dynasty (gilt bronze)
Museum of Fine Arts, Boston

147
Fluted Bowl
Iranian, Sasanian period (silver gilt)
The Cleveland Museum of Art, John L. Severance Fund

We have mentioned above the possible effect of Sasanian silver in stimulating the Chinese potter to improve his wares in order to compete with this new medium, and we pointed to evidences of the Sasanian silver shapes. It is extremely interesting that the form of the vessels, far more than the technique or decoration, interested the Chinese artist, because this aspect of Iranian creativity has similarly had the greatest influence on the art of the West.

The rhyton perhaps provides the most remarkable single instance of this inspiration. The artists of Iran began very early to utilize animal forms in fashioning their vessels. In the earliest levels at Susa, small pots in alabaster were fashioned in the form of animals, and at Level III, about 2000 B.C., at Sialk, we have one of the earliest examples in ceramic. That the Iranian artist should soon have conceived of the idea of combining animal forms with the ancient drinking horn is not therefore surprising. The earliest examples of the horn-shaped rhyton terminating **149** in an animal protoma have been found among the ceramics of Amlash and Kalardasht, which date between 1000 and 800 B.C. The form perhaps reached its highest perfection in the metalwork of the **142** Achaemenid period, and it was probably from Achaemenid Iran that **143** Greek artists derived the form.

148

Tomb relief from Chang-te-fu

Chinese, Northern Ch'i dynasty (rubbing)
Museum of Fine Arts, Boston

Seated figures on the right and left of the center panel are drinking from rhytons.

149
Ewer
Iranian, Amlash, 1000-800 B.C. (ceramic)
Collection M. Foroughi, Tehran

150
Oinochoe
Cypriot, Cypro-Archaic 1, 7th century B.C. (ceramic)
The Metropolitan Museum of Art, The Cesnola Collection, purchased by subscription, 1874-76

151
Ewer with Phoenix Head
Chinese, T'ang dynasty (monochrome lead glaze ware)
Royal Ontario Museum

152
Ewer
Iranian, Kashan, early 13th century (underglaze painted ware)
Royal Ontario Museum

The importance of this motif in the Sasanian period is only now becoming fully apparent as the result of recent spectacular discoveries of Sasanian silver vessels of the highest artistic order. Actual rhytons of this shape have been discovered, and one is illustrated in use on a silver bowl from these same finds. A bronze animal-head support for **144** a rhyton, evidently originally of glass, has long been known from the **147** excavations at Begram in Afghanistan; and a recent discovery by the French Mission at Tepe Khona Masjid, also in Afghanistan, has revealed another interesting one in terra cotta. The Sasanian source of the Chinese form is illustrated in a striking fashion by the incredible tomb reliefs from Chang-te-fu in northern China, dating from the Northern Ch'i dynasty. The reliefs, evidently made for a Sogdian offi- **148** cial in China, represent groups of Sogdians taking part in a series of ceremonial and perhaps ritual scenes. In one of the scenes the central dignitary is drinking from a rhyton of the same form as that illustrated on the Sasanian silver vessel illustrated above. That the Chinese artists of T'ang should have adopted this form is, therefore, not surprising. **145**

The fluted oval bowl, a form evidently invented by the Sasanian silver- **147** smiths, though perhaps derived ultimately from earlier Achaemenid lobed forms, had the most dramatic influence in China. It was copied **146** by the Chinese in silver and in gilded bronze, and in porcelain. Vessels apparently of this shape are also represented in the tomb reliefs mentioned above, and the paintings recently discovered at Pyanjikent near modern Samarkand, in ancient Sogdiana, illustrate another means by which these forms reached the East.

This form, which had such popularity in China, found much less favor in the West where very few examples are known. A single medieval example, carved in semi-precious stone and mounted in gold, is in the Bibliothèque Nationale. A number of renaissance vessels of semi-precious stone in the *Galerie d'Apollon* at the Louvre would seem to be inspired by the same form, but the connections are difficult to explain.

Another striking example of the constant interplay of cultural elements between East and West is provided by the ewer with animal head spout. Undoubtedly a creation of the early Iranian potter and first

153
Ewer
Iranian, Sasanian period (silver)
The Hermitage Museum, Leningrad

known about 1000 B.C. by an example from Amlash, the form traveled to the Mediterranean and is illustrated here by an ewer of the seventh century B.C. from Cyprus. Actual Sasanian examples with an animal head spout have not so far come to light, but the survival of this form in later Islamic ceramics and metalwork leaves no doubt of its existence. A comparison of a Sasanian silver ewer in the Hermitage with one of the many T'ang ceramic versions of this form provides ample proof that the Chinese version was derived from this source. The decoration of many of these T'ang ceramic ewers, as for example, the Sasanian cock turned phoenix and the "Parthian" archer ornamenting the two sides of the ewer illustrated here, is definitely inspired by Iranian work.

The influence of the Iranian metal smith extended beyond the T'ang period. Once again, in the fifteenth and sixteenth centuries, the metalwork of Iran influenced the shapes of Chinese ceramics. A number of blue and white porcelains are known which have forms derived directly from contemporary Near Eastern inlaid brasses, and many with traditional Chinese shapes are obviously modified as a result of this influence. These Near Eastern brasses are precisely the kind that led to the establishment of workshops of Islamic artisans in Venice at the same time.

TEXTILES

The great era of East-West trade in textiles began with the opening of the famous Silk Route across Central Asia by the Han emperor, Wu Ti, about 100 B.C. We know, however, that textiles had been traded between East and West considerably before this date, and it is probable that Iran's role as intermediary had begun just as early as it had in the fields of ceramics and metalwork.

Iranian and Chinese textiles were found together in Scythian graves of the fifth to third centuries B.C. at Pazyryk in southern Siberia, and it is impossible to imagine that, having made the journey thus far, they should not have been exchanged between the capitals of the two great empires of the East and West. When the Chinese ambassador Kang

154
Figured Silk
Chinese, Han period, 1st century B.C.
The Hermitage Museum, Leningrad

155
Silk
Iranian, Sasanian period (compound twill)
The Cleveland Museum of Art, Gift of the Textile
Arts Club

156
Silk

Byzantine Empire (Syria or Egypt), 5th century (compound twill)
The Cooper Union Museum, New York

157
Horyuji Banner

Chinese, T'ang period (silk, compound twill)
Nara, Horyuji Monastery

Ch'ien visited Ferghana in 128 B.C., he reported seeing there "cloth of Su from Szechuan," which the inhabitants told him they had acquired from India. We have no idea what is meant by "cloth of Su," but as silk was the only Chinese textile material of consequence, we may assume that it was some type of silk fabric. At any rate, the statement proves that Chinese textiles had reached the borders of Iran before the actual opening of the Silk Route.

With the opening of the Silk Route we begin to be on firmer historical ground. Besides the considerable Chinese and Western sources concerning this trade, numerous archaeological discoveries provide adequate documentary evidence of the Chinese silks which were first **154** carried over this route.

Although many Western sources have recorded the extravagant use of silk in the late Roman and early Byzantine Empires, we know that it was still rare and a commodity of great luxury at the beginning of the third century A.D. Elagabalus (218-222 A.D.) is said to have been the first Roman emperor to wear a garment wholly of silk. Parthian Iran, as the terminus of the Silk Route across Central Asia, was the chief consumer of the silk which reached its markets, and for a long time that country effectively controlled its further trade with the West. Before Elagabalus' vestments of *holoserica*, silk had been known in the Roman Empire only as an admixture with other textile materials. These partial silks had evidently been woven in the Near East—probably to a large extent in Iran—combining local materials with the more precious imported Chinese silk yarns. This would explain the absence of Chinese influence in the West at this time. We have in this instance one more example of Iran's screening effect on the westward movement of Chinese culture.

Unfortunately the beginnings of the silk weaving industry in the Near East are lost in oblivion, and it is impossible on the basis of the available information to insist on Iran's priority in this field. However, in view of her position of control of the silk trade and by analogy with the history of later periods, we may be sure that she played a key role in the early development of the silk industry and the arts of silk weaving in the Near East. The earliest Near Eastern silks which have come down to us date from the second and third centuries A.D. and

94 were found at Palmyra in northern Syria and Dura-Europus on the Euphrates. In each instance the silk yarns are of Chinese origin, but the technique of the work leaves no doubt that they were woven in the Near East and not in China. It is possible that they could have been woven locally, but as both Palmyra and Dura were primarily caravan cities and not industrial centers, these silks, like the Chinese silks found with them at Palmyra, are most likely imports, and in this case, probably from Iran.

After the fragments of Palmyra and Dura, the first Near Eastern silks which are known appear to date from the fifth and sixth centuries A.D. There are a considerable number of these early silks, which for the most part were preserved as wrappings of relics in European churches but occasionally have come from Egyptian graves. In either case they are quite devoid of any direct evidence of date or provenance but, on

155 the basis of style, they can generally be assigned to Sasanian Persia

156 and to the Byzantine Empire. The silks show a very high level of technical and stylistic development, and they are woven in the same compound twill technique which characterizes all of the great silks of Iran and Byzantium until the end of the tenth century. They were woven on a drawloom that was essentially the same as that which was to be used for silk weaving until the introduction of the powerloom in the nineteenth century.

154 The figured silks of Han, which first traveled the Silk Route, were woven by totally different methods and obviously on quite different looms. These silks, in which the pattern was produced by the warps, were woven on a comparatively simple loom with compensating skill and patience to account for the quality of their designs. In spite of many assertions to the contrary, there can be little doubt that the drawloom was not known in China at this period, and that it was developed in the Near East as a result of the need to adapt the existing weaving techniques to the requirements of the new medium of silk. The fragment from Dura in compound tabby probably marks an early step in this development.

157 The simultaneous appearance of the Near Eastern compound twill technique and Sasanian textile patterns in Chinese textiles of the T'ang period provides adequate evidence of Iran's role in the transmission of this technique to the Far East. The steps by which these patterns and the technique of their weaving reached China are well documented by the quantities of Sasanian textiles, and Chinese copies of them, which have been found at Astana and Ch'ien-fo-tung in Central Asia. The paintings of Pyanjikent and the tomb reliefs at Chang-te-fu, in which we have seen representations of Sasanian silverwork, il-

158
Silk
Iranian, Buyid period, 10th-11th century (diasper weave)
The Cleveland Museum of Art

159
Silk and Gold Textile
Spanish, Islamic period, 14th century (diasper weave)
Cathedral Archives, Salamanca

160

Silk and Gold Textile

Lucca, 14th century (diasper weave)
The Cleveland Museum of Art, Purchase from the
J. H. Wade Fund

161

Silk and Gold Textile

Chinese, Yüan period (diasper weave)
The Cleveland Museum of Art, Purchase from the
J. H. Wade Fund

lustrate the lavish use of Sasanian textiles and demonstrate to what extent the culture of Sasanian Iran dominated that of Central Asia and China in the T'ang period.

The tremendous impact which the Sasanian textile art had on the Far East was very nearly paralleled in the West. Long after the end of the Sasanian period, characteristic Sasanian textile motifs continued to dominate Byzantine textile patterns. From the end of the eleventh century there is the example of the great "elephant silk" at Aachen, made in the royal *zeuxippos* at Byzantium, clearly derived from an Iranian prototype such as one in the Louvre which belonged to Abu Mansour Bukhtakin, Kaïd of Khorassan, d. 961 A.D. The same pattern was carried farther west, to Spain, where it occurs not only in textiles but also **159** in sculpture of the Romanesque period. There can be little doubt of Iran's role as a creative force in the development of the textile arts of both East and West in the early Middle Ages.

However, as we have seen in the other media, both ceramic and metal, there was a constant interplay of the influences moving between East and West. The influence of one cultural element never moved long in one direction before being countered by one moving the other way. The art of Sasanian Iran—particularly silver and textiles —dominated the decorative arts of T'ang, but soon, in early Islamic times, it was the T'ang ceramics moving back over the same trade route which were to have such a profound effect on the development of the ceramic art of Islamic Iran and ultimately that of the entire Western world. There was a parallel movement of Chinese textiles which influenced, perhaps not so dramatically, the textile arts of the early Islamic period in Iran and probably the rest of the Near East.

We know from many Arabic and Persian sources how extensively Chinese textiles were used and how highly they were esteemed in this period. The compound twills of the Near East, by the necessity of their technique, were thick, heavy weaves. Patterns were achieved by changing the colors of the various parts of the design; the richer the polychromy, the heavier and thicker the silks became. If the great elaborate patterns that could be achieved in this technique fascinated the Chinese, so the soft, delicate character of Chinese damask must have fascinated the weavers of Iran. It was probably under this influence that the next great technical step in the evolution of silk weaving was taken in Iran in the tenth century.

In 1928 a large number of silks were found in tombs on the hill of Nakkara Khaneh, outside Rayy, the capital of Buyid and early Seljuk Iran. Among the silks, of which a number were dated to the late tenth and early eleventh centuries, were compound twills in the Sasanian technique and Chinese damasks, but the majority were woven in a new technique, called "diasper" or, in the language of the weavers of Lyons, "lampas". Most significant among these diasper weaves were a **163** number that illustrate experimental stages by which the weavers of Iran arrived at this new technique. The silk fragment shown in figure 158 illustrates this experimental stage. The Chinese influence in the cranes and the bamboo stalk of the tree in the interstitial motif is quite obvious. The development of the diasper—or lampas—technique was the result of further improvements on the drawloom which made possible the formation of patterns through contrast in texture between background and design. Very large-scale, complex designs such as those woven in compound twill could be produced with the minimum of material, resulting in very light and elegant textiles such as the two examples illustrated. This technique, carried by Islamic weavers from Iran to Spain and on to Italy, later dominated the entire textile art of medieval Europe and was the basis for all further development of the silk weaving industry in the Near East and in Europe until power looms in the nineteenth century brought an end to weaving as an art. Again, the technique of diasper found its way back to China where we know it at least as early as the Yüan period.

In all these cases technical influences are of paramount importance, though attendant stylistic factors are far from negligible. We have noted already to what extent the T'ang textiles were influenced by both the technique and the style of Sasanian silks. The Chinese influence, both technical and stylistic, on the silks of the Buyid period can be further illustrated by one or two concrete examples. The phoenix on the T'ang ewer, which is almost identically reproduced on a T'ang silk from Ch'ien-fo-tung, was unquestionably influenced by the Sasanian cock, as we can judge from its representation on the tomb relief from Chang-te-fu. The phoenix, as we know it in Chinese textiles of the Yüan period, was also a common motif on Iranian ceramics—and we may assume textiles, although none are known— of the Mongol period, and it became a popular motif in Italian textiles of the fourteenth century, where probably it was derived more directly by way of Mamluke textiles of Egypt which were, of course, in turn influenced by the art of Mongol Iran.

(Margin numbers: 159, 160, 161, 151, 148, 161, 129, 162)

162
Silk and Gold Textile
Lucca, 14th century (diasper weave)
The Cooper Union Museum

163
Silk

Iranian, Buyid period, 11th century (diasper weave)
The Cleveland Museum of Art, Purchase from the
J. H. Wade Fund

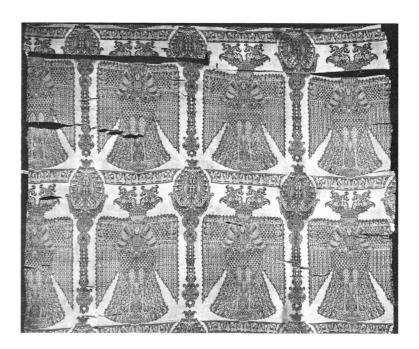

164
Silk

Chinese, Macao, 16th century (diasper weave)
The Metropolitan Museum of Art, Rogers Fund, 1912

165
Silk

Spanish, 12th century (compound twill)
The Cleveland Museum of Art, Purchase from the
J. H. Wade Fund

166
Bowl

Iranian, Sasanian period (silver)
Mahboubian Gallery, New York

One of the most amusing and exaggerated examples of cultural diffusion is the motif of the double-headed eagle. Perhaps a weaver's invention, because the symmetrical duplication of the head offered an easy solution to a technical problem, the double-headed eagle is found several times among the textiles from Rayy, and it was often **163** copied by the weavers of Byzantium and Spain. It was undoubtedly **165** from one of these sources that the coat of arms of the Hapsburgs and later the kings of Spain were derived. This motif became a popular one in the sixteenth century Spanish textiles, and from here it found its way to Macao to be copied by Chinese weavers for export to **164** Portugal.

The grapevine often found on Chinese textiles is another important motif which has moved back and forth between East and West, by way of Iran, for the best part of two thousand years. The origins of the grapevine as a decorative motif in the art of the Classical world and the Near East are lost in antiquity. Its greatest exploitation was probably during the Hellenistic period in Greece and the Near East, where it served as a symbol of the cult of Dionysus, and was used with almost fanatical abandon on everything from wine cups to architectural decoration and sarcophagi. From this source Sasanian Iran adopted the motif, where evidently through a synthesis of the Hellenistic cult of Dionysus and the Iranian cult of Anahita, the vine became the symbol of that goddess and at the same time became synonymous with the *homa* of the Avesta. It occurs endlessly in Sasanian art, particularly on **144** silver vessels probably used for wine-drinking rites, such as those il- **147** lustrated in Pyanjikent paintings and the tomb reliefs of Chang-te-fu. **166** Although we know that it was Kang Ch'ien who first introduced the grapevine into China on returning from his mission to Ferghana, the vine was not finally adopted as a decorative motif in China until the **167** T'ang period, under the influence of the art of Central Asia and Sasanian Iran.

167
Mirror
Chinese, T'ang period (bronze)
The Cleveland Museum of Art, Dudley P. Allen Fund

FOR FURTHER READING

SPECIAL REFERENCES

N. Barnard, *Bronze Casting and Bronze Alloys in Ancient China*, (Canberra, Monumenta Serica Monog. XIV, 1961).

G. Brett, "West-East", *Bull. of the Royal Ontario Museum of Archaeology*, no. 2 (October, 1953).

————, "East-West," *Bull. of the Royal Ontario Museum of Archaeology*, no. 19 (September, 1959).

H. Garner, *Chinese and Japanese Cloisonné Enamels*, London, 1962.

————, "The use of imported and native cobalt blue in Chinese Blue and White", *Oriental Art* (Summer, 1956).

Bo Gyllensvärd, "T'ang Silver and Gold," *Bull. of the Museum of Far Eastern Art*, no. 29 (1957), pp. 1-230.

R. Soame Jenyns and Wm. Watson, *Chinese Art*, New York, 1963, p. 11, Pl. 9.

GENERAL

A. J. Arberry, *The Legacy of Persia*, Oxford, 1953.

R. Ghirshman, *Persia from the Origins to Alexander the Great*, Thames and Hudson, 1964.

————, *Iran, Parthians and Sasanians*, Thames and Hudson, 1962.

A. Godard, *L' Art de l'Iran*, Paris, 1962.

Wm. Honey, *The Ceramic Art of China and Other Countries of the Far East*, London, 1945.

A. Lane, *Early Islamic Pottery*, London, 1947.

B. Laufer, *Sino-Iranica* (Field Museum of Natural History, pub. 201, Anthropological Series, vol. XV, no. 3, Chicago, 1919).

VI

Cultural and Artistic Interchanges in Modern Times

THEODORE BOWIE:

DIFFUSION AND EXCHANGE OF IDEAS, FORMS, TECHNIQUES, AND MATERIALS HAVING TO DO WITH ART HAVE PREVAILED, ALMOST WITHOUT INTERRUPTION, BETWEEN EAST AND WEST for three thousand years, if not longer. It is hard to determine which side is in debt to the other: the balance appears to be even, but the probability is that, at least since the sixteenth century, the West owes more to the East. The older, overland contacts, broken by the interposition of Islam, were re-established by sea on what is called the Spice Route.

The West has been, and continues to be, an enthusiastic importer of Eastern objects of art. The overwhelming mass of the objects collected, up to very recent times, however, belong in the category of curios or works of *virtu*—silks, ceramics, jades, ivories, jewelry, and the like. Such pieces are usually small and easily transportable; they possess artistic qualities, not the least of which is exquisite craftsmanship. Many Eastern techniques were imitated and adapted in Europe, and in the eighteenth century a set of hybrid styles grew up in the domains of architecture, gardening, furniture-making, and the decorative arts generally. The terms *chinoiserie* and *turquerie,* and later *japonaiserie,* were applied to the style which produced some extremely remarkable creations. But the success of the style was undoubtedly due, at least in part, to the affinity of late baroque and rococo manner of the eighteenth century in the West for the ornate and florid nature of Ming and Ch'ing, Mughal, and Tokugawa, of which most of the imported articles were representatives. There was some sort of equivalent coincidental movement in the East for which the term *occidenterie* has been proposed, but it was a rather sporadic phenomenon. China was clearly more interested in Western medicine and mathematics than in its arts; India was largely indifferent (except for some Mughal rulers); and Japan remained obdurately closed to all foreign influences after a brief lifting of its curtain.

What stands out is the fact that among the masses of artifacts which poured into the West almost no paintings and no sculpture reached Western lands. Such nonutilitarian productions began to be imported only well after 1850. Painting, sculpture—and architecture—are commonly regarded as the embodiment and repository of undefiled aesthetic values, but the practitioners of those arts across the world have been very late in absorbing each other's values. In the rest of this chapter we will discuss some recent instances which may suggest the beginnings of an understanding on the part of artists in one tradition of the aesthetic values of another.

The problem of architectural influences cannot be treated adequately here. The West may possibly be indebted to the East for the concept —and the technique—of the pointed arch and perhaps of the high dome. We have undoubtedly borrowed numerous other ideas from various parts of Asia; in the eighteenth and nineteenth centuries Chinese gardens enjoyed a great vogue in England and on the continent. At the present time Japanese domestic architecture and the kind of garden arrangement influenced by Zen ideas are very popular, especially in America. Japanese architects today are adapting Western

168

169

methods and are helping to create a true international style.

Sculpture, the premier art of much of Asia, is still very inadequately known in the West and has had little influence. Rodin is the only sculptor on record to have expressed fulsome admiration for certain late Indian pieces. And while Hellenistic and Roman statuary had a definite impact on Indian craftsmen working in the region of Gandhara in the second and third centuries, the hybrid Gandhara form had less effect on the development of classical Indian sculpture in India proper than on that of Buddhist images in Central Asia, China, Korea, and Japan. The imprint of Greece is still perceptible in those remote regions after many centuries, but sometimes it takes a specialist to make it out.

Has Western painting been influenced by Eastern concepts? It is worth trying to find a valid answer to this question because of the special importance which we accord to painting as the art form expressing the subtlest and most meaningful values; historically China and Japan have shared this attitude, so that the problem of Western influences on Eastern painting is equally challenging.

168

Illustration from *Suite de Jeu Chinois*
Drawing by J. B. Pillement, 1728-1808, engraved by M. de Monchy about 1775
Cooper Union Museum

169

Painted and Printed Cotton Hanging
Madras, 1755
Cooper Union Museum

The central design is the Chinese Tree of Life, while the borders are in the Western tradition.

170

Winter and Summer
Italian, 18th century (polychrome terracotta)
Wadsworth Atheneum, Hartford

Some fifty years ago Bernard Berenson suggested that there was something Chinese about the style of Sienese painting; Simone Martini and others, he felt, might have seen some Chinese works. This connection is very difficult to document, but other scholars claimed to see Eastern influences in Tuscan art and elsewhere. With a little bit of imagination one can make much of the obvious affinities that exist between Leonardo's theories and practice and those of certain painters of the Sung period. Asian personages appearing in the works of Uccello and Pisanello look more convincingly Eastern than the numerous Magi who represented the East in numerous Adorations because they are actual individuals seen by the artists in the flesh rather than images copied from some painting. The Bellinis and Tintoretto reflect Venetian contacts with the Levant and the Ottoman Empire. In the seventeeth century, during the period of Dutch trade with the Indies, Rembrandt and his contemporaries discovered Persian and Indian miniatures.

171

172

Boucher and Liotard, in the eighteenth century, were attracted by China and Turkey respectively, and Delacroix and Fromentin, among others of the nineteenth century, steeped themselves in the North African aspect of the Orient. But none of these exposures were of lasting significance. Delacroix, who traveled about North Africa for a few weeks, brought back a new concept of local color, but nothing of profoundly significant aesthetic nature. Jacopo Bellini and Liotard, who each spent more than four years in Turkey, did not bring anything back which constituted a turning point in Western painting.

Orientalism and Exoticism are strong impulses which undoubtedly lead to certain kinds of renewal in Western art, best typified by Gauguin's flight toward Primitivism. But none of these examples reaches to the heart of the matter, that is, whether or not Western thought and Eastern, particularly Far Eastern, ideals in painting have begun to unite in a meaningful and aesthetically significant manner. And although painting seems to be the one art form in which there is common ground for an artistic meeting at a profound level, yet the dialogue has barely been engaged. The Orient which we see reflected in European painting from the time of the Renaissance on is Levantine, which is to say Arabic and Islamic. It is brilliantly colorful in its trappings and backgrounds; and it rapidly breaks down into a set of conventions. When China becomes popular, we find the same stress

172
Asia, by W. Chr. Mayer
Berlin, about 1770 (porcelain)
Cooper Union Museum

171
Painted and Printed Cotton Hanging
Indian, second half of the 18th century
Cooper Union Museum

The Indian manufacturers working for the Dutch trade used Chinese and Japanese designs.

173
Chinese Gentleman and Attendant
Meissen, about 1760 (porcelain)
Herron Museum of Art, Indianapolis

174
Tea Caddy, by William Cripps
London, 1772-73 (silver)
Cooper Union Museum

175
Tôle Glass Holder
French, about 1765
Cooper Union Museum

on gaudy externals, with a touch of quaintness. In no case has the East really revealed itself to the West, for the simple reason that no personal or intimate work of art that might give any clue to the soul of the East was sent forth. Had Carpini or William of Rubruk or Marco Polo brought back a single painting, and had Leonardo or any other Italian artist had the opportunity of unrolling that scroll and meditating upon it, we might have some reason for considering the influence of China on Western art. But even today the European painter is very largely ignorant of the full scope of Chinese and Japanese painting: there are very few collections, either public or private, except for a small number of European museums whose holdings do not begin to compare with those in the United States.

The only time that any of Oriental art had a significant impact on Western painting was the period between 1865 and 1900 when artists like Whistler, Degas, Lautrec, Manet, Van Gogh, and a few others collected Japanese prints and profited from the lessons in composition, design, and tonal relationships which could be taught by what was, in Japanese eyes, a minor branch of their art. But when European painting took a new turn under the guidance of Cézanne, the appeal of the Orient seemed to come to an end. In the twentieth century very few European artists, other than Klee or Matisse, have evinced much interest in the subject or reflect an important Eastern influence in their work.

American artists have reacted somewhat differently. In the first place, the United States showed an interest in collecting works of art—as distinguished from the kinds of objects that were the normal staple of China trade—much earlier than elsewhere in the Western world, and this interest was more persistently cultivated. The Museum of Fine Arts in Boston set an example which had tremendous influence on other American museums. The Metropolitan, the Philadelphia, the Freer, the Cleveland Museums, the Art Institute of Chicago, the William Rockhill Nelson Gallery in Kansas City, and the Fogg (to cite only those which come readily to mind) contain collections of Oriental art of prime quality which have been constantly enriched. Should world

176

Fountain, attributed to Wan Chen-p'eng

Chinese, first part of the 13th century (detail from Ta-Ming Palace Scroll)
John M. Crawford, Jr., Collection, New York

This fountain is possibly related to the one constructed for Kublai Khan's predecessor by a French goldsmith named Guillaume Boucher, who had been captured by the Mongols at the Siege of Belgrade and transported to Karakorum.

177

Portrait of the Emperor K'ang Hsi

Engraving in Hazart, Catholisches Christenthum, *Vienna, 1678-1725*
Lilly Rare Book Library, Indiana University

The Manchu Emperor K'ang Hsi (1662-1722) was an enlightened patron of the arts with a very friendly attitude toward Western ideas in architecture and painting.

178

View of Jehol, by Father Matteo Ripa

From The 36 Views of Jehol, about 1724 (etching on copper)
New York Public Library

The Jesuit Father Ripa was urged by Emperor K'ang Hsi to make 36 views of the Summer Palace at Jehol (north of Peking) in a medium in which he had no practice whatever and for which the suitable tools and materials were lacking. These etchings, which measure 12 inches by 13½ inches, are undoubtedly the first copper etchings ever made in China. The Emperor was delighted with them and distributed sets to all his relatives.

179

View of the Château d'Eau, by an anonymous Chinese artist

1783 (copper-plate engraving)
New York Public Library

K'ang Hsi's second successor was Ch'ien-lung (1736-1795), a name equally famous in art. Ch'ien-lung caused another Jesuit, Father Giuseppe Castiglione, to design and build, in the French style, a set of buildings known as the Yuan-Ming-Yuan or Summer Palace. Father Castiglione, who painted in the Chinese manner under the name of Lang Shih-ning, trained the Chinese artists who made these large copper engravings, measuring roughly 20 inches by 30 inches.

conditions prevent scholars from working directly in Asia, valuable work could still be done on the basis of what is available in this country. And artists have unequalled opportunities for frequent and prolonged contacts with superb examples of Oriental art in every conceivable medium. What is more, we have had both the interest and the means to induce various Eastern countries to send out some of their national treasures of art on tour to American museums. Such circulating exhibitions touch Europe only infrequently. Finally there has been a certain amount of official and quasi-official aid in helping students and artists to travel and work in the Orient.

We ought now to begin to detect traces of the influence of Oriental art in the work of some Americans. Yet outside of a handful of potters and such painters as Mark Tobey, Morris Graves, Ulfert Wilke, Walter Barker, and not many others, such traces are not very perceptible. One artist, Ad Reinhardt, whose work shows no ostensible sign of an orientalizing manner, has developed a philosophy of art strongly affected by Chinese aesthetic theory. He has had a very scholarly introduction to the subject. What effect his views may have on his contemporaries is an open question.

On the other side of the world, the reaction of the four major countries—Iran, India, China, and Japan—to Western art has not followed any consistent pattern. With the exception of Japan, they seem to know practically nothing of the subject and have never shown much interest in pursuing it. Certainly China has always been open-minded about borrowing forms, techniques, and materials from external sources, as numerous examples in this book demonstrate. And the

180

The Conquests of Ch'ien-lung, by Charles-Nicolas Cochin fils
French, 1715-1790 (engraving)
Library of Congress

Sixteen paintings celebrating Ch'ien-lung's victories, done in the Chinese style, were copied by four Jesuit missionaries for engraving in Italy. Through a series of intrigues the drawings arrived in France and were assigned to the foremost engraver of the time, the younger Cochin. The work took ten years, and the original edition consisted of 200 prints of each of the sixteen subjects. The dimensions are roughly 20 inches by 30 inches.

181
Blue and White Vase
Chinese, K'ang Hsi period (porcelain)
John Pope Collection, Washington, D.C.

The Chinese version of a Delft medicinal jar. The production of Delft blue ware had originally begun as an imitation of Ming blue-and-white ware.

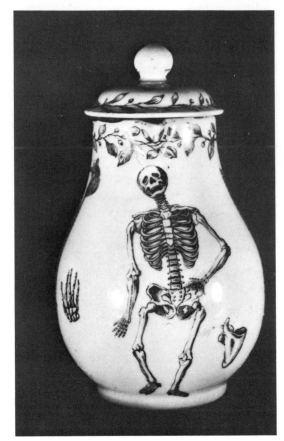

182
Creamer
Chinese, Ch'ien-lung period (porcelain)
Mrs. Elinor Gordon, Villanova, Pennsylvania

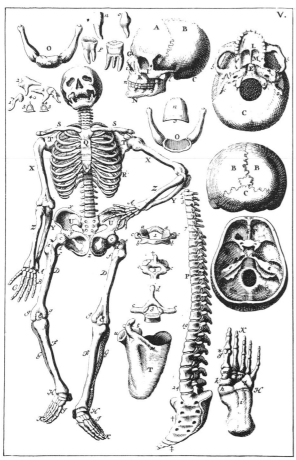

183
Anatomical Drawings
From Kulmus, Anatomische Tabellen, *Leipzig, 1759*
Indiana University Fine Arts Library

184
Bowl with Designs of Dutchmen and Dutch Vessels
Japanese, 18th century (Imari ware)
Seattle Art Museum, Eugene Fuller Memorial Collection

185
Octagonal Dishes
(left) Japanese, 18th century (Kakiemon ware)
(right) Meissen, 18th century
John Pope Collection

186
One of a Pair of "Foreigner" Screens
Japanese, Momoyama period, 1573-1615 (color and gold on paper)
The Cleveland Museum of Art, Leonard C. Hanna, Jr., Bequest

187
Mendez Pinto
Japanese, 19th century (ivory netsuke)
Seattle Art Museum, Eugene Fuller Memorial Collection

Gyokuyosai, a Japanese carver active in the early part of the nineteenth century, depicted the first European to land in Japan in the form of a Chinese scholar with a mythical *kilin* or unicorn at his feet. The presumed date of Fernando Mendez Pinto's landing, July 5, 1539, is incised on the back.

Chinese anticipations of Western painting, discussed earlier in this book, should at the very least have predisposed a few Chinese painters in favor of Western aesthetic practices if not theories.

The Buddhistic style of painting, which gives prominence to the human form rendered in terms of volume by the manipulation of color and chiaroscuro, has remote Western ties. The style was introduced into China about the fourth century, reached a high point of development during the T'ang period, and completed a final stage of evolution in Japan between the seventh and the twelfth centuries. Forms created in Central Asia, themselves connected with both the Indian and the Hellenistic traditions, gave birth to this type of painting which, in essence, was contrary to the Chinese linear tradition. When Buddhism ceased to be of significance, painting addressed itself to a very small and almost private audience and was an expression of Taoist philosophy akin to, and in fact intimately connected with, poetry.

The insular and isolationist Japanese have been far more ready than the Chinese to accept radically new artistic ideas. In spite of the fact that the Taoist conception of painting prevailed there from at least the fifteenth century on, in 1799 a little book called *Seiyo Gadan* was published in Tokyo. Shiba Kokan, its author, was a painter who had become familiar with Western ways while living in Nagasaki. A Dutch trader gave him a copy of Gerard de Lairesse's *Schilderkonst* (known in English as *The Art of Painting*). This was a revelation to him: the imitation of reality for which the Western artist strove seemed to him more serious and meaningful than what he called the Chinese and Japanese "playful avocation" with the brush, and the solidity of oil technique far superior to water-color. European tricks of perspective, three-dimensionality, chiaroscuro, and other devices made the home product look like "children's scratches." *(Cont. on page 128)*

188

Ancient Roman Ruins, by Hokkuju

Japanese, ca. 1835 (woodblock print)
Robert Laurent Collection, Bloomington

An engraving of one of G. P. Pannini's famous paintings showing a rearrangement of the ruins of Rome undoubtedly reached Japan in the latter part of the eighteenth century, because the first version of it in a Japanese print was made by Toyoharu. This version is much lighter and has cloud effects essayed by Hokkuju.

189

The Colossus of Rhodes, by Kunitora

Japanese, ca. 1862-65 (woodblock print)
The Art Institute of Chicago, Emily Crane Chadbourne Collection

190
Allegorical Figure by Mantegna, copied by an anonymous Indian artist
16th century (?)
Stuart Cary Welch Collection, Cambridge

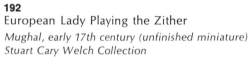

191
Portuguese Gentleman and Indian Lady
Mughal, ca. 1570 (miniature painting)
Stuart Cary Welch Collection

192
European Lady Playing the Zither
Mughal, early 17th century (unfinished miniature)
Stuart Cary Welch Collection

193
Presentation Scene
Mughal, early 17th century (unfinished miniature)
Stuart Cary Welch Collection

194

The Siamese Embassy at the Court of Louis XIV

Engraving in Tachard, Voyage de Siam, *Paris, 1686*
Lilly Rare Book Library, Indiana University

195

Three French Noblemen on Horseback

Siamese, early 18th century (gold leaf on black lacquer)
From the Lacquer Pavilion in the Suan Pakkad Palace, Bangkok

During the middle of the seventeenth century the principal minister of the King of Siam was a Greek named Constant Phaulkon. He induced his master to open relations with European powers. The engraving shows a Siamese Embassy bringing presents to Louis XIV, who is receiving them in the Hall of Mirrors in palace at Versailles in 1684. This business was long suspected of being a hoax perpetrated to amuse the Sun King, but there is ample historical evidence that this was a genuine mission. Louis XIV responded three years later by sending the Chevalier de Chaumont to the Siamese monarch at Ayuthia. It is presumably he and his companions who are represented as witnessing the "Victory over Mara" scene depicted in this panel. The presence of foreigners during the major events of the Buddha's life is frequently observed in Buddhist art.

Cultural and Artistic Interchanges in Modern Times **/ 119**

196

The Nestorian Inscription
(rubbing)
The Fogg Art Museum, Cambridge

In the year 781, in the city of Chang-an (now known as Siking), there was erected a stone slab about nine feet high and three feet wide, on which were carved 1780 Chinese characters. This text commemorates the introduction of a Christian doctrine in China in the year 635, under the protection of T'ai-Tsung, the great founder of the T'ang dynasty. The particular doctrine propagated in China is that of Nestorius, Patriarch of Constantinople in the early part of the fifth century. The Council of Ephesus rejected as heretical his idea that Jesus Christ was the perfect union of a divine and a human person. Nestorianism flourished in China until the year 845.

197

Madonna and Child
Chinese, probably 18th century
(porcelain, Te-hua ware)
Royal Ontario Museum

199

Cross

From Sinkiang or Inner Mongolia, 14th century (bronze)
Royal Ontario Museum

There was a brief revival of Christianity in China under the protection of the Yüan dynasty, and it is presumed that crosses such as this one, which may have been ornamented with enamel or semi-precious stones, belong to that period.

198

Crucifix

Chinese, late Ming dynasty (ivory)
Ralph M. Chait Collection

Both of these carvings in the full round (each approximately nine inches high), were presumably done by Chinese craftsmen from models brought by Jesuits after 1580. The Child is clearly the work of a man who understood sculpture, whereas the maker of the Crucifix, who must have worked from a painting, exaggerated the relief of muscles and blood vessels.

199

200

Christ Child

Chinese, Ming dynasty (ivory)
Ralph M. Chait Collection, New York

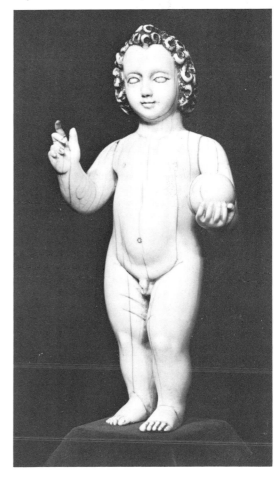

201
Madonna and Child
Illustration from Matteo Ricci's Commentaries on
the Precious Pictures, *Peking, 1606*
Princeton University Library

Father Ricci's commentary is in Chinese and Roman-
ized characters. The illustrations were redrawn by
Chinese artists from sixteenth century engravings by
such engravers as Wierix and Van de Passe.

202
Madonna and Child
Mughal, probably 17th century (miniature)
The Fogg Art Museum

203
A Bishop
Turkish, about 1600 (miniature on marbelized paper)
The Museum of Fine Arts, Boston

204
Indian Falconer and Archer, by Rembrandt
Dutch, 1606-1669 (drawing)
The Pierpont Morgan Library

Many Mughal miniatures were imported into Holland in the seventeenth century. Rembrandt once owned two dozen, which he copied in sketches of this type.

207
Head of a Bird, by Edouard Manet
French, 1875 (lithograph)
The Art Institute of Chicago

208
Duck, by Hokusai
Japanese, ca. 1840 (sumi sketch)
The Art Institute of Chicago

206
Tall Bridge, by J. McN. Whistler
American, 1878 (lithoprint)
The Art Institute of Chicago

205
Ryogoku Bridge, by Ando Hiroshige
Japanese, 1831 (woodblock print)
The Art Institute of Chicago

Whistler learned from the Japanese that any kind of mood could be established by the use of decorative tones and patterns at the expense of three-dimensional illusion. This becomes an Eastern technique abstracted by Western artists in an analytical way that would have been utterly alien to the originators.

207

208

209
Ghost of Sara Yashiki, by Hokusai
Japanese, ca. 1820 (woodblock print)
The Art Institute of Chicago

That greatest of Japanese realists, Hokusai, was an equally powerful evoker of phantasms. Redon, who specialized in surrealistic visions, had a natural affinity for this side of Japanese art.

210
Sea Anemone, by Odilon Redon
Lithograph for Les Origines, *1883*
The Art Institute of Chicago

211
Aux Ambassadeurs, by Toulouse-Lautrec
French, 1894 (lithograph)
The Art Institute of Chicago

213
Boating, by Pierre Bonnard
French, 1897 (color lithograph)
The Art Institute of Chicago

212
La Coiffure, by Mary Cassatt
American, 1891 (dry-point, soft ground and aqua-tint)
The Art Institute of Chicago

214
Young Woman Silhouetted Against the Shore,
by Edvard Munch
Norwegian, 1899 (woodcut)
The Art Institute of Chicago

215

Ceremonial Bronze Taking the Form of a Bird,
by Morris Graves

American, 1947 (water-color)
The Seattle Art Museum, Gift of Mr. and Mrs. Philip Padelford

Many ceremonial bronzes of the Shang period are zoomorphic; bird forms are frequently used. Graves reverses the process here.

216

Lady Apart, by Paul Klee

Swiss, 1940 (brush and ink drawing)
The Museum of Modern Art, New York

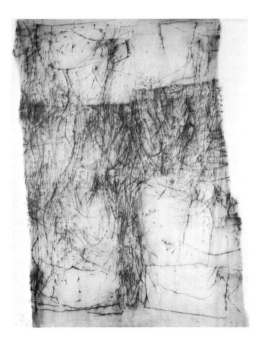

217

I-Ching Series No. 5, by Walter Barker

American, 1963 (oil)
The Museum of Modern Art, Gift of Mr. and Mrs. Morton D. Day

The peculiar calligraphic language used by this contemporary American painter is derived from the ancient Chinese practice of scapulimancy, a ritual divination that interprets the cracks made in sheep's shoulder-blades which have been placed in the fire. The *I-Ching* or "Book of Changes," formulated during the Shang dynasty, gave the key to the oracles.

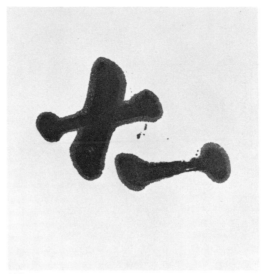

218

Plus and Minus, by Ulfert Wilke

American, 1958 (sumi)
Collection of the artist

Ulfert Wilke, who teaches painting at Rutgers University, spent the year 1958-59 in Japan and resided for a time in a Zen temple in Kyoto.

219

Black Flute, by Mark Tobey

American, 1953 (tempera)
The Willard Gallery, New York

Tobey spent some time in Japan, under the instruction of a Zen master. Taken literally, this is a calligraphic depiction of a cobra rising out of its basket at the sound of its master's flute. Other levels of meaning remain closed to the uninitiated.

Since such disrespect for Taoist ideals could have been regarded by the government as treasonable and subject to rigorous punishment, we cannot know whether Shiba Kokan's book reached many of his compatriots. Several Ukiyo-e print artists such as Toyoharu, Hokusai, and Hiroshige, and Masanobu before them, had adapted, more or less awkwardly, Western ideas of perspective. Maruyama Okyo had even gone so far as to invent a kind of camera viewer faintly reminiscent of Dürer's. He also analyzed schematically the human nude. But no large group of practicing artists turned to the West wholeheartedly until after 1868, when some artists not only took up a foreign method but totally rejected native traditions in concept, style, technique, and materials.

220
Lagoons, by Henri Matisse
French, from Jazz, 1947 (découpage and collage)
Indiana University Art Museum

To Matisse the Orient was at first the classic Levantine world bordering on the Mediterranean. In his
later development, he gives much evidence of having been influenced by Persian miniatures. The technique and forms used in *Jazz* are strongly reminiscent also of the effects found in Islamic decorative
art, based on the use of tiles with brilliant glazes.

It is very difficult for any Westerner imbued with admiration for the
older Japanese forms to express a fair opinion about this Westernized
art. Enormous talent is evident in the production of this school—and
little originality. It is very depressing to go through Japanese galleries
and museums and observe the local version of every Western style
from that of the Impressionists to that of the latest pop and op man.
Only in the medium of the print, which has had a real rebirth, and in
the mode of abstract expressionism, where the Japanese have succeeded in giving a national air to a form which has become so international as to lose all character, do we see exciting results from a
Western inspiration.

221
A Scene in Holland, by Utagawa Toyoharu
Japanese, 1735-1814 (woodblock print)
The Art Institute of Chicago

Like many of his fellow artists, Toyoharu was in-
trigued by Western treatment of perspective and
chiaroscuro effects, but it is evident that he had not
fully mastered their principles.

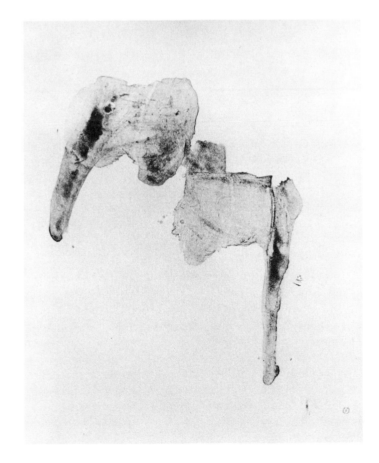

222
Abstract Calligraphy, by Nankoku Hadai
Contemporary Japanese
Collection of Ulfert Wilke, New York

The Japanese have begun to follow the Western
craze for calligraphy without regard to esoteric
meanings. In "action writing," a very close parallel
to "action painting," the character of the brush
stroke is the main value.

130 / *East-West in Art*

223
Bombardement Incessant, by Wallasse Ting
Contemporary Chinese, 1959
(oil painting on canvas)
The Detroit Institute of Arts

Born in China in 1929, the artist first went to France
but is now working in the United States.

224
Landscape with Bird, by Kenzo Okada
Contemporary Japanese (painting on screen)
The Herron Museum of Art

Kenzo Okada lives in the United States now.

225
Shoji, by Kyoshi Saito
Contemporary Japanese, 1954 (woodblock print)
The Art Institute of Chicago

226
Main Street, by Takahashi Shinichi
Contemporary Japanese, 1959 (woodblock print)
The Art Institute of Chicago

The influence of Kirchner, Mondrian, and others is plainly visible in these works, which yet succeed in preserving the native idiom.

227
Evening Sun, by Yoshio Fujimaki
Contemporary Japanese, 1934 (woodblock print)
The Art Institute of Chicago

228

229

230

THREE WORKS BY ISAMU NOGUCHI

228
Jomon
1962 (granite)
Cordier and Ekstrom, New York

229
Big Boy
1952 (Karatsu ware)
The Museum of Modern Art

230
Bird C (Mu)
1952-53 (Greek marble)
The Museum of Modern Art

A *nisei* born in Los Angeles, Noguchi had the advantage of being trained both in the United States and in Japan. His work is the most convincing proof that a perfect balance between Eastern and Western traditions can be achieved.

In the last fifty years a few Japanese collectors have been able to acquire some fairly good examples of Western art, mostly of the modern period; in postwar years Japan has been able to import a few circulating exhibitions of Western art, and to send a few Japanese artists and students abroad. On the whole, however, the Japanese expatriates have had the best opportunity for harmonizing the aesthetics of the East and the West, provided always that they have received a thorough grounding in one tradition before approaching the other. The mere fact of being an Oriental by birth is no guarantee of special artistic insight, or we would have had far more Nisei painters.

The presence of the British in India and of the French in Southeast Asia did not result in a deeper awareness of Western art in those lands. Peoples there knew masterpieces of Western art through books and reproductions if at all. Under the influence of a few Western teachers and artists native artists often would treat traditional themes in a Westernized manner. Even the encouragement of revival of native arts and crafts has at times been marked by ill-advised incitement to appeal to a specious Western market. Here, as in China and Japan, the possibility of fusing two aesthetic modes depends upon the development of a number of powerful artists—or even a single strong original talent—who are at home in both traditions.

In general mutual East-West artistic influences, even during the second half of the twentieth century, are meager and not excessively vigorous in nature. In a sense, the early Western attempts, through missionaries and merchants, to infiltrate Asia with its artistic ideas and productions is a forerunner of the contemporary phenomenon which is the Westernization, or Americanization of that continent. This development has not had happy results, for the most part, and what we are learning from the Orient (as for instance in Japanese architecture and design) is of much greater quality and substance than what they are learning from us, so far as we can see.

FOR FURTHER READING

ON ARTISTIC INFLUENCES

B. Berenson, *Essays in the Study of Sienese Painting*, 1918.

C. R. Boxer, *Jan Compagnie in Japan, 1600-1850*, 1950.

R. C. Craven, Jr., "A Short Report on Contemporary Painting in India," *Art Journal*, v. 24, no. 3 (Spring, 1965), 226-233.

L. Olschki, "Asiatic Exoticism in Italian Art of the Early Renaissance," *Art Bulletin* (1944), 95 ff.

I. V. Pouzyna, *La Chine, l'Italie et les Débuts de la Renaissance*, 1935.

Ad Reinhardt, "Timeless in Asia," *Art News* (January, 1960).

————, "Twelve Rules for a New Academy," *Art News* (May, 1957).

G. Soulier, *Les Influences Orientales dans la Peinture Toscane*, 1924.

O. Statler, *Modern Japanese Prints: An Art Reborn*, 1956.

Also, the Fall, 1958, issue of the *College Art Journal* (v. xviii, no. 1) is devoted almost entirely to discussions of various aspects of relationship in art between East and West, with articles and letters by Joseph Campbell, Hugo Munsterberg, Ulfert Wilke, and others.

ON CULTURAL INTERCHANGES

C. R. Boxer, *Fidalgos in the Far East*, 1947.

Hugh Honour, *Chinoiserie*, 1961.

Clay Lancaster, *The Japanese Influence in America*, 1963.

A. C. Moule, *Christians in Asia before the Year 1550*, 1930.

L. Olschki, *Guillaume Boucher, a French Artist at the Court of the Khans*, 1946.

P. Pelliot, *Influences Européennes sur l'Art Chinois au 17e et au 18e Siècle*, 1948.

S. C. Welch, "Early Mughal Miniature Paintings," *Ars Orientalis*, v.3, 1959, pp. 133-146.

Royal Ontario Museum, Toronto, *East-West*, 1952, and *West-East*, 1953, catalogues of exhibitions with texts by Gerard Brett, F. S. G. Spendlove and Helen Fernald.

Musée Cernuschi, Paris, *Orient-Occident, Rencontres et Influences durant Cinquante Siècles d'Art*, 1958-59. Catalogue of an exhibition sponsored by UNESCO, with texts by V. Elisséeff, R. Bloch, J. Auboyer, C. Sterling and others.

VII

RICHARD B. REED:

A Bibliography of Discovery

THE GREAT PERIOD OF EUROPEAN EXPLORATIONS IN THE FIF-TEENTH AND SIXTEENTH CENTURIES OWED MUCH OF ITS STIMULUS TO THE IDEAS OF THE CLASSICAL AND MEDIEVAL geographers and cosmographers of the Mediterranean world—Pomponius Mela, Pliny the Younger, Strabo, Solinus, Macrobius, and Ptolemaeus. These authors possessed a fragmentary and at best conjectural knowledge of the world, and their writings about the Far East were scanty and highly imaginative. But with the exception of a few travel narratives, the Renaissance voyageur had little else on which to base speculation about the world beyond his immediate ken.

"Le Livre des Merveilles du Monde" (in the Pierpont Morgan Library) is a beautiful example of a fifteenth-century compendium of information derived from ancient and medieval writers such as Solinus, Marbode, Pliny, and Orosius. The manuscript, presumably made for René d'Anjou, contains fifty-seven illuminations attributed to Jean Fouquet, whose representations of scenes and persons in the Near East and farther Asia (i.e., "Scythia") are, at times, fairly accurate and at others, entirely fanciful.

The popular *Cosmographia* of Pomponius Mela, first printed in 1471, went through more than twenty-five editions before the middle of the sixteenth century. The Salamanca edition of 1498 contains a world map and several pages devoted to India and the Arabic lands. Solinus' *Polyhistor* circulated widely in manuscript form before it was printed in 1473. It is an accumulation of misinformation regarding mythical and marvelous creatures of nature, although in succeeding editions, more reliable materials were incorporated. In the Basle, 1538, imprint, there are a number of woodcut maps, including one of the world which indicates some of the Portuguese activity in the Indian Ocean.

While the works of the classical writers maintained a continued popularity and influence, another form of literature—the travel narrative—really caught the enthusiasm of the literate European in the fifteenth and the sixteenth centuries, and the most important and influential traveler of all was Marco Polo. Although his famous "Book of Marvels" was treated with some skepticism when it was written in the early years of the fourteenth century, it circulated widely in numerous manuscript translations, and survived to become one of the most celebrated accounts of Asia ever written. Polo's graphic descriptions of the wonders of the Orient inspired the adventurers of the age of discovery, and despite some exaggeration, his basically truthful observations provided a fairly accurate account of the mysterious lands of Asia. Prince Henry the Navigator possessed a manuscript copy, and Christopher Columbus owned, and heavily annotated, the first Latin edition.

A number of the manuscript copies of Marco Polo's itinerary have survived. "Le livre des merveilles d'Asie" (France, fourteenth century), in the Pierpont Morgan Library, is a fine example of late fourteenth-century illumination, and contains a number of interesting miniatures depicting places and important events relating to the travels of Marco Polo. The first printed edition of Polo's book appeared in German with the title *Das puch des edelñ Ritters vñ landtfarers Marcho*

231

The Meeting of East and West

An illumination from Le Livre des Merveilles du Monde, *French, 1450 or earlier*
The Pierpont Morgan Library

This work should not be confused with the *Livre des Merveilles* belonging to the Bibliothèque Nationale in Paris and dating from the latter part of the fourteenth century, which includes the relation of voyages by Marco Polo, Odoric da Pordenone, and Mandeville.

232

Imaginary Portrait of Marco Polo

Frontispiece of the first printed edition of his account, Das puch . . . des Marcho Polo, *Nuremberg, 1477*
Lilly Rare Book Library, Indiana University

233

The Land of the Seres, or China

An illumination from Le Livre des Merveilles du Monde
The Pierpont Morgan Library

234

A Map of the World

From Pomponius Mela, Cosmographia, *Spanish incunabulum, 1471*
Lilly Rare Book Library, Indiana University

235

A Page from the Manuscript of *Le Livre des Merveilles de l'Asie*

Written and illuminated in Picardy, probably at the end of the 14th century, containing Marco Polo's relation of his voyages
The Pierpont Morgan Library

The page is the beginning of Chapter XXXV, in which Marco Polo describes how he was sent by the Chinese Emperor to the point, ten miles out of Cambaluc, the capital, where there is a bridge over the river Pulisanghin. This river flows out to sea; at the time it was a very active channel of trade.

Polo (Nuremberg, 1477). The more popular, and more widely read first Latin version was printed at Gouda in 1483: *De cõsuetudinibus et cõdicionibus orientaliũ regionũ*. Succeeding editions and translations incorporated new information as it became known, but the original text was not altered substantially and remains even today as a tribute to the veracity and keen judgment of the author.

The most controversial travel book of the Middle Ages was the amazing compilation attributed to the enigmatic John de Mandeville. Written some time during the fourteenth century, this mixture of fact and fancy thoroughly delighted the contemporary European. The author remains unknown, despite numerous attempts to identify him, and it is not even certain that he actually did any of the traveling for which he makes such extravagant claims. The book is replete with wonderful figments of the author's imagination, interspersed liberally with descriptions taken from other sources, primarily Odoric of Pordenone's *Descriptio Orientalium Partium* and the works of Wilhelm von Boldensele and John of Plano Carpini, as well as the classical writers. The German edition, *Reysen und Wanderschafften durch das Gelobte Land* (Strassburg, 1483), contains a number of woodcuts testifying to the prevailing readiness to accept such fantasies as real.

In an entirely different vein from Mandeville, yet a part of the imaginative literature of the Middle Ages, is the fable of Barlaam and Josaphat, attributed to Saint John of Damascus, a Syrian monk who lived in the eighth century. The story in effect translates into Christian terms the life of Buddha, or more particularly the *jataka* tales. This popular book was translated into almost every European language (including Icelandic, in the fourteenth century) before it was printed in 1471. The first German edition, printed in Augsburg in 1476, is also the first illustrated edition. Many of the sixty-four woodcuts testify to the closeness of the parallel between the Indian and the Christian versions of the story of the incarnation.

The works of the Greek astronomer, geographer, and mathematician, Ptolemaeus (second century A.D.) provided an important bridge between the two periods of geographical thought. Renaissance geographers, while adopting his concepts almost without change, drew maps to accompany his text, which incorporated contemporary advances in knowledge in contradiction with Ptolemaeus.

Many Ptolemaic misconceptions, however, such as the enclosed Indian Ocean, were not dispelled until the monumental voyages of Bartolomé Dias and Vasco da Gama. His idea of the great southern continent, *Terra Australis,* inspired the European explorer until the time of Cook's voyages in the eighteenth century. And, perhaps most important, his erroneous estimate of the length of a degree was a prime factor in Columbus' decision to seek a westward route to India.

The most famous of the fifteenth-century editions of Ptolemaeus is the *Cosmographie* printed at Ulm in 1482, the first edition to contain information derived from the Portuguese explorations along the west coast of Africa. Johann von Armheim, who is believed to have designed the world map in this edition, reflects the prevailing European dependence on Ptolemaeus and Marco Polo. The continually re-

236

Map of the World

From Ptolemy's Cosmographie, *Ulm, 1482*
Lilly Rare Book Library, Indiana University

This is one of the most famous maps in the history
of mapmaking. It was printed from woodcuts and
colored by hand. The indication at the top states
that it was engraved by Johanne Schnitzer de
Armssheim.

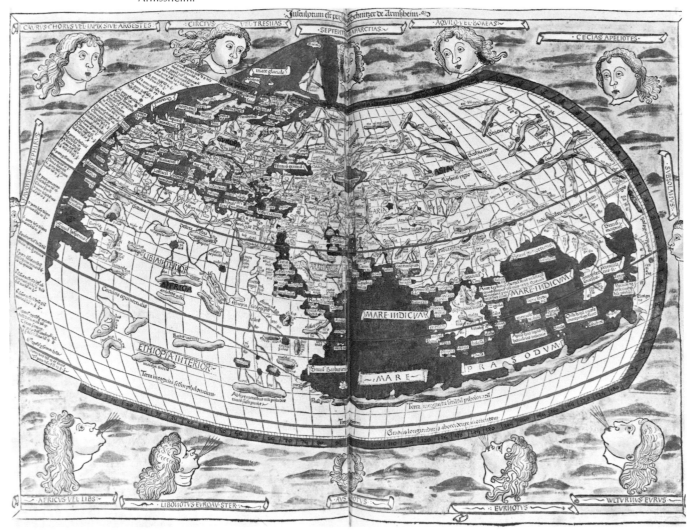

237

Josaphat's First Outing

A page from the first German printed edition of
Barlaam and Josaphat, *Augsburg, 1476*
The New York Public Library, Spencer Collection

The engraving shows Prince Josaphat (the name is
a corruption of the Indian word "Bodhisattva") as
he meets a beggar, a cripple, and a blind man in
the course of an outing, an adventure which defeats
his father's purpose in shielding him from all knowledge of the world's evil. The composition of the
scene is very similar to the same episode in the life
of Prince Gautama, the future Buddha, as rendered
by ancient Indian sculptors. There is no possibility,
however, that the German artist could ever have
been aware of this.

vised maps in the many editions of Ptolemaeus that were produced
before 1600 give a graphic history of that dynamic age of discovery.

By the end of the fifteenth century the art of printing, combined with
improved techniques of illustration, made possible the production of
an extraordinary compilation by Hartman Schedel, *Registrum huius
operis libri cronicarum cu figuris et ymagibus ab inicio mudi* (Nuremberg, 1493), more familiarly known as the "Nuremberg Chronicle."
The work is remarkable for the profusion of woodcut illustrations depicting almost every figure of any importance since the beginning of
recorded history: Alexander, Tamerlane, and Darius of Persia are
included, along with the fanciful and mythical creatures of the East
that continued to haunt the European mind. The *Novissime hystori-
arum* (Venice, 1503) of Jacopo Filippo Foresti, another chronicle
similar to Schedel's, contains brief descriptions of the cities and towns
of the known world, with a number of woodcut views including Constantinople and Odessa.

The *Secondo cãtare dell india* (Rome, 1494-95) by Bishop Giuliano
Dati, the celebrated translator of the Columbus Letter, recreates the
exotic lands of the East in verse. A number of woodcut illustrations
describe the strange—often nonexistent—beasts that inhabited the
East. Only four copies of this little book are known, a fact which might
indicate the popularity and hard use that it enjoyed at the time.

The sixteenth century was the great century of European expansion.
The book that had the most influence initially, and which contributed
most to publicizing this movement was *Paesi novamente retrouati*
(Vicenza, 1507) by Fracanzano da Montalboddo. Fifteen editions
were printed between 1507 and 1528. Its primary emphasis was the
New World, but the voyages and discoveries of Vasco da Gama and
Pedro Alvares Cabral to India were included. The clear, methodical,
and accurate presentation in this book made a tremendous contribution to geographical knowledge. The purpose of the *Paesi* was to
inform, and it did so admirably. But in spite of these revelations of the
discoverers and explorers many Europeans continued to believe in the
mythical and grotesque inhabitants of far-off lands. The woodcut engraving of dog-headed cannibals on the title page of Lorenz Fries'
Underweisung und uszlegunge Der Cartha Marina oder die mer carte
(Strassburg, 1530) is eloquent testimony to this persistence.

The sixteenth century saw the establishment of Portuguese power in
the Indian Ocean. It was the era of Vasco da Gama, Afonso de Albuquerque, João de Castro, and Luis de Camões. Portuguese literature
reached its greatest heights, in the narrative chronicle and the epic
poem. João de Barros, outstanding chronicler of the Portuguese empire, wrote a classic of Portuguese prose, which is absolutely indispensable for the study of the search for the route to India and the
establishment of the empire in the first half of the sixteenth century.
Asia (Lisbon and Madrid, 1552-1615) was written in four "Decades."
The first covers the Portuguese voyages from the time of Prince Henry
through Vasco da Gama and the appointment of Francisco de Almeida
as viceroy of India. In the second, the work of Almeida and the great
Afonso de Albuquerque is described. The establishment of the Portu-

guese in Southeast Asia and the East Indies is the subject of the third, and the fourth, which was not published until 1615, relates the history of the empire through the seige of Diu in 1538.

Barros' work was continued by Diego do Couto, who wrote eight more "Decades," including another fourth. The entire eleven "Decades" were finally printed together in 1778. Couto, having spent a good part of his life in India as keeper of the archives at Goa, was a worthy successor to Barros, and taken together, their works are the foundation of our historical knowledge of the Portuguese Empire in the sixteenth century.

Another exceptional historian, Fernão Lopes de Castanheda, went to India in 1528, and spent several years traveling throughout the empire. His *Historia do descobrimento e conquista da India pelos Portuguezes* was first published in Coimbra from 1551 to 1561. Since it initially preceded Barros' *Asia,* the work enjoyed a wide reputation, and the first volume soon appeared in French (1553), Spanish (1554), Italian (1556), and English (1582) translations. Castanheda did not concern himself with the African voyages, but concentrated on the period from Vasco da Gama to João de Castro. His history, while lacking the flair of Barros, nevertheless is informative, accurate, and valuable.

The account of the most celebrated Portuguese traveler in Asia, Fernão Mendes Pinto, was long considered suspect. The *Peregrinaçam* (Lisbon, 1614) describes the journeys of this extraordinary traveler through China, Japan, Southeast Asia, and the islands from 1537 to 1558. Pinto was among the first Europeans to visit Japan, in 1542, and for a time acted as a companion to Saint Francis Xavier. His *Peregrinaçam* is now accepted as authentic and fairly accurate.

238
The Island of Ceylon
Wash drawing from the manuscript of Lizuart de Abreu's Cousas Raras de India, *composed in 1558*
The Pierpont Morgan Library

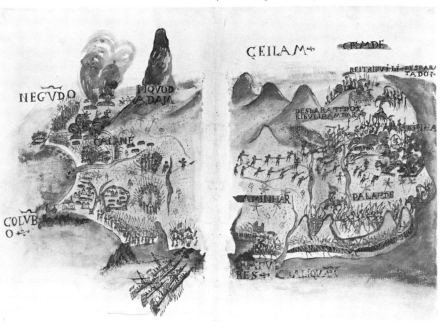

The Portuguese Empire in Asia reached its height in the middle of the sixteenth century, and the man most closely identified with this success was João de Castro, a veteran of many battles in the Near East and India. He traveled extensively throughout the Portuguese possessions on the Indian subcontinent, and later was appointed viceroy in 1548, shortly before his death. To raise money for the rehabilitation of Diu in 1545, he pledged his beard as security to the merchants of Goa—a gesture which has gained him considerable fame. Castro's career has been chronicled by Jacinto Freire de Andrade in his *Vida de Dom João de Castro quarto Viso-Rey da India* (Lisbon, 1651).

Only the epic poet, Luis Vaz de Camões, surpasses these great prose chroniclers in the Portuguese literature of discovery. His epic in the classical style, *Os Lusiadas* (Lisbon, 1572), is the supreme tribute to a glorious century of empire. The subject is the voyage of Vasco da Gama, but the theme is the greatness of Portugal. His story in verse has an aura of authenticity since he had spent many years in the East in the service of the crown.

The world chronicle remained popular and informative well into the sixteenth century. Antoine du Pinet's *Plantz, pourtraitz et descriptions de plusieurs villes et forteresses, tant de l'Europe, Asie, & Afrique, que des Indes, & terres neuves* (Lyons, 1564) was a collection of views, maps, portraits, and scenes relating to all of the major areas of the world. The world map in this volume, and the one in Abraham Ortelius' *Theatrum orbis terrarum* (Antwerp, 1570), graphically represent the advances in the cartographic knowledge concerning Asia in the half-century since serious European interest in that part of the world developed.

As in the New World, the missionary societies—and most prominently, the Society of Jesus—played an important role in the gathering of information and the observation of the people of the East. The letters that the Jesuit fathers sent back to their superiors in Rome and other European cities are a fantastically rich source of information. Appended to Francisco Alvarez' *Historia de las cosas de Ethiopia* (Zaragoza, 1561) is an extremely important series of letters written by Jesuit missionaries in the Far East and Brazil: *Copia de diversas Cartas de Algunos padres y hermanos de la compañia de Jesus . . . en las Indias del Rey de Portugal, y en el Reyno d'Japon, en la tierra de Brasil. Con la description d'las varias leyes, y costumbres de la gente del gran Reyno de la China.* It includes seven letters (one of which reports the death of Saint Francis Xavier) describing activities of the Order and customs and events in China and Japan. The *Rerum a Societate Iesu in Oriente* (Cologne, 1574), a valuable source of letters compiled by Giovanni Pietro Maffei, is, in addition, one of the first European books to contain printed Japanese script. Luis Froes wrote a long and most important letter, which contains a valuable account of Japan, published in the collection, *Brevis Iapaniae insulae descriptio* (Cologne, 1582).

The *Historia de las cosas mas notables, ritos y costumbres, del gran Reyno dela China* (Rome, 1585) by Juan González de Mendoza became the standard European classic on China for more than a century

239

Camoens' Cave at Macao

From an engraving in Sir George Staunton, An Authentic Account of an Embassy from the King of Great Britain to the Emperor of China, *London, 1797 Princeton University Library*

There is a tradition that Camoens spent a considerable length of time in Macao, composing the *Lusiads* at the spot which bears his name today.

240
Map of the World
From Antoine du Pinet, Plantz, Pourtraitz . . ., *Lyon, 1564*
Lilly Rare Book Library, Indiana University

after its publication. It was the first European book to reproduce Chinese characters in print. It went through numerous editions and translations in the sixteenth and seventeenth centuries, including an English edition translated by Robert Parke with the title of *The Historie of the great and mightie kingdome of China* (London, 1588).

The English reading public was not truly familiar with literature on the East until 1577 when *The History of Travayle in the West and East Indies* (London) was published. This work was actually an expanded edition of Richard Eden's *Decades of the Newe Worlde* (London, 1555), completed after Eden's death in 1576 by Richard Willes. Willes added accounts of Anthony Jenkinson's travels in Russia and the Middle East, Ludovico di Varthema's "Itinerary" through the Near East and into India, Galeotto Pereira's description of China, and selections from Maffei's Jesuit letters from Japan.

The great English achievement in geographical literature, Richard Hakluyt's monumental collections of voyages and travels, was published in the last decade of the sixteenth century. Although this outstanding Elizabethan did not travel and explore himself, he probably

Illustrations from Theodore de Bry, Petits Voyages, parts xi and xii, ca. 1628
Lilly Rare Book Library, Indiana University

241
The Siege of Bramaputra by the Grand Khan of Tartary in 1608

242
Javanese Dancers

243
A Japanese Temple with Guardian Divinities

contributed more to enlightening his contemporaries concerning English overseas activity than did any other single individual. He was an indefatigable translator, collector, and propagandist, and dedicated himself to promoting the cause of English exploration and colonization throughout the world.

The Principall Navigations, Voiages, and Discoveries of the English Nation (London, 1589), published in one volume, was divided into three sections, the first two of which concerned Asia. He described the voyages of John Newberry and Ralph Fitch to India in 1583, the travels of Anthony Jenkinson in the 1550's and 1560's, and included several narratives of journeys made by representatives of the Muscovy Company into Persia and surrounding areas.

A second, and even more magnificent edition came out in three volumes, from 1598 to 1600. It followed the same format, but contained a vastly increased amount of information, including the voyages of Cesar Frederick to the East Indies, Thomas Stevens to Goa in 1579, and a number of documents relating to English activities in the East.

When Richard Hakluyt died in 1616, Samuel Purchas, an inferior man by comparison, continued to collect narratives of voyages and travels, and in 1625, published in four volumes, *Hakluytus Posthumus, or Purchas His Pilgrimes, Contayning a History of the World in Sea Voyages and Land Travells by Englishmen and Others* (London). The genius of Hakluyt's organization and prose is missing, but Purchas did add a number of important accounts, not only of Englishmen but other nationalities as well: the journal of John Saris' voyage to the Moluccas and Japan, Sir Thomas Roe's embassy to the Great Mogol, Edmund Scott's discourse on Java, the travels of Anthony Sherley in

244

Brahmanism and Mohammedanism Face to Face in India

Illustration from Linschoten, Discours of Voyages, London, 1598

Persia, and the letters of Nicolas Pimenta from India are among the most important.

At the same time, in Frankfort, Germany, the De Bry family began the publication of a most elaborate and ambitious collection of voyages and travels, embellished throughout with engravings of maps and scenes. For general purposes the set may be divdied into two series: the *Grands Voyages,* concerning America; and the parts on Asia and Africa, the *Petits Voyages,* in small folio, issued in thirteen parts, in Latin and German, published between 1597 and 1628. The *Petits Voyages* contain narratives of expeditions made by Linschoten, Cornelis de Houtman, Jacob Cornelisz, Wybrandt van Warwijck, Jacob van Neck, Joris van Spilbergen, and Willem Barentsz, among others.

Toward the end of the sixteenth century, the Dutch began their intrusions into the Portuguese East Indies. The most famous, and by far the most important, of the Dutch writers was Jan Huygen van Linschoten, who sailed to India in 1585. His *Itinerario* (Amsterdam, 1596) links him with Hakluyt, the propagandist, although Linschoten's ideas were reinforced by actual observation. His work was translated into English as a *Discours of Voyages into ye Easte & West Indies* (London, 1598). Linschoten's fellow Dutch pilots looked upon his work as a practical navigational manual with detailed descriptions of the routes into the East Indies and beyond. Linschoten shrewdly perceived the weaknesses of the Portuguese, and pointed out opportunities for his own countrymen to strengthen the Dutch position in the East.

The geographical literature of the seventeenth and eighteenth centuries did not differ too much from that written earlier. Collections, travel accounts, atlases, and chronicles continued to amaze, delight, and inform the European populace, but tended to be more sober and informative, and less conjectural and speculative. The sumptuousness of the publications of the Blaeus, Van der Aa, and Hulsius compensate, in part, for any decline in brilliance of writing.

The large number of woodcut illustrations of various peoples such as the Tatars, Indians, Chinese, Persians, other Eastern natives lend special value to Hermann Fabronius' *Newe Summarische Welt Historia* (1612). This comprehensive world history emphasizes Asia.

Melchisedec Thévenot has frequently been called the French Hakluyt, and his collection, *Relations de divers voyages curieux* (Paris, 1663-1672), in four parts, seems worthy of a place alongside that of the more famous Englishman. Thévenot took the entire world as his province, and the voyages and travels of men of all nations as his subject. Among the narratives relating to Asia, he included that of Grueber and d'Orville to China, Méthold's voyage to the Gulf of Bengal in 1619, the travels of Anthony Jenkinson, the memoirs of Thomas Roe, the descriptions of China by Martin and Boym, and the Dutch accounts of China by Nieuhof.

The history of the Roman Catholic Church throughout the world was written by Cornelius Hazart in his *Catholisches Christenthum* (Vienna, 1678-1725), published in three volumes. Based primarily upon the letters of the Jesuits and other missionaries, it contains a wealth of information on the activities of the various orders, and is illustrated with a number of engravings depicting scenes of martyrdom in the Far East.

During the second half of the seventeenth century a number of French journals and accounts of travels to Southeast Asia were published. Guy Tachard's *Voyage de Siam, des pères Jesuites* (Paris, 1686-1689), in two volumes, relates the voyage of six Jesuits around the Cape of Good Hope, through the islands of the East Indies, and on to Siam. The *Relation de l'ambassade de Mr. le Chevalier de Chaumont à la cour du Roy de Siam* (Paris, 1686) is an account of an embassy sent by Louis XIV to the King of Siam, and contains several illustrations, including a folding plate of the royal barge. Like Chaumont, Simon de la Loubère was a special ambassador to the Siamese court, but he left a much more detailed description of life in Siam in his *Du Royaume de Siam . . . en 1687 & 1688* (Paris, 1691). He wrote on such diverse topics as Asian astronomy and mathematics, the Siamese language, and chess and smoking.

In 1696 Louis Le Comte, a Jesuit, published his *Nouveaux Mémoires sur l'Etat de la Chine*, which was issued the next year in an English translation as *Memoirs and observations . . . Made in a late journey through the emipre of China* (London, 1697). The author had been sent to China in 1685. His book is written in the form of a series of letters addressed to important persons in Europe, but is a detailed study of the country and people of China. At the time Le Comte was accused of a complete lack of objectivity in his laudatory account of Chinese

245
The King of Siam on his State Elephant
Illustration from Tachard, Voyage de Siam, *Paris, 1686-89*
Lilly Rare Book Library, Indiana University

civilization: copies of his book were ordered destroyed by the authorities in Paris.

One of the most elaborate and important sources for the study of the Chinese Empire was written by another Jesuit, Jean Baptiste Du Halde, working in Rome primarily from missionaries' letters. The *Description géographique, historique, chronologique, politique, et physique de l'empire de la Chine et de la Tartarie Chinoise,* first published in Paris in 1735 and reprinted the next year at La Haye in four volumes with an atlas, still remains one of the best accounts of the Chinese people in the eighteenth century.

In 1668, the French physician C. Dellon began a decade of traveling in the East that eventually took him through the islands of the Indies to Goa where he was condemned for heresy by the Inquisition and banished from the Portuguese possessions. His valuable account of his voyages, published in English as *A voyage to the East-Indies* (2 vols; London, 1698), reveals the author as a perceptive observer of the life

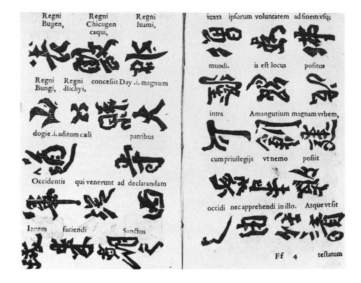

246
A page of Japanese characters
From Maffei's Rerum a Societate Yesu in Oriente, *Cologne, 1574*
Lilly Rare Book Library, Indiana University

and customs of both Europeans and Asians. He describes numerous native illnesses and their remedies.

In 1692 Peter the Great, who looked to the East as well as to the West, sent Everard Ysbrants Ides, a Dane, on an overland mission to Peking. The nearly three years that the journey occupied afforded him ample opportunity to record his impressions of the country and its people. His book was translated into English under the title, *Three years travels from Moscow over-land to China* (London, 1706).

The great Dutch scholar Nicolaas Witsen wrote an exhaustive work on the land of the Tatars: *Noort ooster gedeelte van Asia en Europa* (Amsterdam, 1705), in two volumes. The engraved illustrations depicting scenes of almost every aspect of Chinese life as well as natural phenomena and plans of cities, and a number of maps, combined with Witsen's authoritative text, contribute to making this book an indispensable source.

William Coxe's *Account of the Russian Discoveries between Asia and America* (London, 1780) dwells particularly on the Russian voyages in the north Pacific and to Alaska, but does describe, in less detail, Russian interest in Siberia and Muscovy-China relations. There are several large folding maps and plates, including a detailed map of Siberia and the Russian Empire.

In spite of the availability of these many basically truthful accounts of the East, the eighteenth-century European was still fascinated by the mystery of the East. Capitalizing on this mistaken but enthusiastic attitude, a rather capricious young man hit upon the idea of posing as an Oriental who had been converted to Christianity and succeeded for a while in one of the most amazing literary hoaxes of the age. George Psalmanazar was a Frenchman who became a naturalized English citizen living under an assumed name. He first posed as a Japanese convert but later called himself Formosan. He invented a language

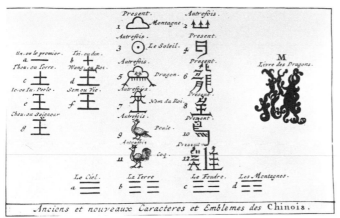

247

Some Ancient and Modern Chinese Characters

Illustrations from the four volumes of the
Galerie Agréable du Monde *devoted to Asia*
Published in Leiden by Pieter van der Aa, 1729
Lilly Rare Book Library, Indiana University

249

The Pepper Tree Plantation in the East Indies

248

The Daimyo's Palace in Miyako (Kyoto)

Representation du Temple où l'on voit Idole de 300 Mains, en Japon.

TEMPEL met Duysend BEELDEN.
TEMPEL with a thousand Images.

250
The Temple of the Thousand Idols (unquestionably the Sanjusangendo in Kyoto)

Illustrations from the four volumes of the Galerie Agréable du Monde devoted to Asia
Published in Leiden by Pieter van der Aa, 1729
Lilly Rare Book Library, Indiana University

251
Japanese Divinities,
including Amida

252
The God Brahma

253
A Parsee Funeral Tower

Illustrations from Volume I of *Cérémonies and
Coutumes Religieuses,* Leiden, 1789
Lilly Rare Book Library, Indiana University

254
Temple of the Goddess Kwan Yin in China

and a religion to aid in his deception and, at the height of his fame, published *An historical and geographical description of Formosa* (London, 1704), partly to silence the numerous challenges to his veracity. Since he had never been further east than Germany, Psalmanazar's account was based on other written sources, and on his own vivid imagination. Eventually he repented his deceptions and passed into a rather uneventful retirement.

In 1789 *Cérémonies et Coutumes Religieuses de tous les Peuples du Monde* was published in Amsterdam, under the imprint of Laporte, with one of its four volumes entirely devoted to Asia. Engravings by Bernard Picard dominate the work, which has very little text. By relying too heavily on many of his Dutch predecessors, Picard perpetuated a number of misconceptions and plain misstatements of fact in his plates of fairly high artistic quality. The work is an interesting reflection of the anti-religious spirit of the times.

With the growth of archaeological research in the nineteenth century, the reports and descriptions of Asia tend to become more scientific and less receptive to legends and fables. A new period dawned in which the wide-eyed wonderment which characterizes many of the books described in this chapter is replaced by the detachment of the scholar.

FOR FURTHER READING

E. Bretschneider, *Mediaeval Researches from Eastern Asiatic Sources*, 1887.

M. Letts, *Mandeville's Travels*, 1953.

B. Penrose, *Travel and Discovery in the Renaissance, 1420-1620*, 1952.

A. T'Serstevens, *Les Précurseurs de Marco Polo*, 1959.

Yule and Cordier, *The Book of Ser Marco Polo*, 1920.

VIII

DENIS SINOR:

Foreigner—Barbarian—Monster

ALTHOUGH MAN IS A SOCIAL ANIMAL, THE NATURE OF THE BONDS HOLDING HUMAN GROUPS TOGETHER REMAINS ALMOST COMPLETELY UNKNOWN. IN MOST CASES, THE ULTIMATE reasons why an individual joins one group rather than another are as unclear as are the criteria by which he is admitted into or rejected by a group already in existence. The motives that create a feeling of solidarity among members of the same group govern our daily life but remain elusive. Any one human being has an inborn sense of his own identity, but a group of human beings can attain group identity only by comparing itself with other groups. A human community gains independent existence by differing in some respect from other communities.

But what are the criteria that underlie these distinctions? They are of necessity subjective and arbitrary: there is no natural distinction between man and man. Skin color may matter in some parts of the world, but not in others. Language can be, but is not always, an important link. England and the United States are separate states even though English is spoken in both countries; Switzerland is a united nation but it is multilingual. Geographical boundaries are certainly not "natural"; the English of Northern Ireland are more "English" than are the Scots living in Great Britain. Such distinctions are man-made; they lack universal validity.

Whatever the initial reason for cohabitation, human groups develop behavioral patterns of their own. These patterns are extremely complex and affect every aspect of human life, from economic activity to religious thinking. Although the elements in the composition of several patterns may be identical, each combination of them is unique and forms what could loosely be called a civilization. It would be idle to speculate here on the factors which separated various civilizations in the beginning. The earliest historical evidence reveals considerable differences between the behavioral patterns of the various human groups. These, in their turn, tend to widen other gaps already existing between the groups. From the point of view of an outside observer, there may seem to be no difference between the two tribes, A and B, living in close neighborly relations, in analogous physical environment and in similar economic conditions, and yet members of both groups are very conscious of all-important differences: tribe A's totem-animal is the stork and B's, the eagle. The differences between Lutherans and Catholics may have seemed insignificant to a sixteenth-century Chinese and yet caused bitter battles between the two groups. What matters in one century is often unimportant in another. What is essential and what is not will be judged differently according to time and place, but the feeling of solidarity among men having the same criteria for what is "essential" will always appear among members of the group. Theoretically, adherence to a given group is a voluntary, subjective act. In practice, however, most men are born into the community in which they will spend all their lives, not only because they will meet no alternatives, but also because, having been conditioned to the prevailing set of values in the community of their birth, they will instinctively recoil from a different behavioral pattern.

Most members of most human groups honestly and deeply believe that their set of values is the best, that the criteria they have chosen are essential, in short, that their "civilization" is the finest, if not the only one worthy of the name. They will look with suspicion and even open hostility on anyone who would come to them from a different community—a foreigner.

But the foreigner has an important role; his mere presence suffices to give birth or new life to group-consciousness. He is someone to gaze at, to laugh at. He is different, surprising, unexpected, even comical. Is he a man? No doubt, since he has a head, two eyes, two legs, and is man-sized. But can he speak? Or is he *niemci*, i.e., "mute," as the Germans were to the Slavs. If he speaks, does he do it "frankly," understandably, as do the Franks?

> The Stranger within my gate,
> He may be true or kind,
> But he does not talk my talk—
> I cannot feel his mind. . . .

In these lines, Kipling echoes a thought more forcefully expressed by Saint Augustine: "For if two meet . . . and neither can understand the other, you may sooner make two brute beasts of two several kinds sociable to one another than these two men . . . . So that a man rather be with his own dog, than with another man of a strange language."

Even if the Foreigner does not speak differently, is not his cloth ridiculous? To wear a garb is a privilege. Not every one may don the uniform of, for instance, a general. But it is also a duty; in most societies cloth will show the wearer's place, his rank in the world. Is it not the cowl that makes the monk? The Foreigner is strangely dressed. He may button his garment on the right, when all others, i.e., the Chinese, button theirs on the left. He may wear a cap which does not show at first sight his rank; he may even have headgear which he would not be entitled to wear. "Well ordered are the garments and headgear," says a Chinese inscription, to show that everything is under control, in good order. Shame on the Roman who wears Barbarian cloth, shame on the King of Hungary who—in the thirteenth century—was bitterly reproached by the Pope for wearing his hair and his clothes in Turkic fashion.

As long as the Foreigner is alone he may be mocked at, and if he is not apologetic, he may even be disliked. But the time may come when the Foreigner becomes a Barbarian; instead of a curiosity, he is a menace, primarily because he is no longer alone. The Foreigner is acceptable as long as he comes to China, Byzantium, or Washington, modestly offering his presents which the Ruler with fatherly benevolence, deigns to accept. But when Foreigners become too numerous and audacious, they may become Barbarians who, forgetful of their own status which would prescribe quiet reserve, think that the world belongs to them, and together with their own, and on civilized soil, "sing, arm in arm, and will speak of their homeland."

What the Barbarian most lacks are manners. He does not know how to behave. He acts "without propriety," lament the Greeks; in the Chinese Book of Ceremonies, rules of conduct differentiate between

255
Cynocephali
Woodblock illustration from the first German edition of Mandeville's Voyage and Travel, *printed in Strasbourg in 1483*
New York Public Library, Spencer Collection

The concept of a human with a dog's head is a universal one. Mandeville describes these *cynocephali* as "inhabitants of the isle known as Macumeran who have heads like hounds. They are reasonable and worship an oxe for their god. They all go naked, but for a little cloth around their privy members; they are good men to fight." Macumeran, or Natumeran, has been identified as one of the Nicobar Islands in the Indian Ocean.

A Garland of Monsters
Woodblock illustrations, by Wolgemut, for Schedel's Nuremberg Chronicle, *1493 Lilly Rare Book Library, Indiana University*

256
One of the "Mysteros," with eyes in their shoulders and a mouth in their breast

257
One of the Scythian "Pannotii," with ears reaching down to the ground

258
A "hippopede"

259
A "sciopod," with his foot large enough to shade him from the sun

the Civilized Man and the Barbarian: "to follow the inclinations is the way of the Barbarian." "They are called Barbarians," says Albertus Magnus in the thirteenth century, "who are not ordered for virtue by law or government or the discipline of any other system." If order is good and disorder is bad, is it not the duty of the Civilized Man to impose his order on the Barbarian? But what is this order? How could a Barbarian ever become civilized?

The Barbarian is necessary, however. His contradictions of Civilization help to define the Civilized Man. Each has a role to fulfill: "Inside are those who don the cap and the girdle [the Chinese]; outside are the Barbarians." They live beyond the pale, in the Outer Darkness; they are evil by nature. Thus to conquer the Barbarian is an act of virtue. "For the Civilized conquers as a free man and establishes liberty, whereas the Barbarian, a slave by nature, can only enslave . . ."—a monstrous idea clearly still held by Montesquieu. According to Roger Bacon the antithesis of the Barbarian is the "rational being." The Barbarian has no rights and what he owns is not his; his property or authority is usurped from others. He must be kept at bay like the wild animals. He must be hunted or enclosed.

Indeed, the typical Barbarian, the archenemy of human order—of the establishment—is enclosed: he belongs to the impure people of Gog and Magog. How fortunate we are that some hero—in the Western tradition, Alexander the Great—shut them behind impenetrable mountains. "He remembered the wicked nations, which dwelt in the ends of the earth, and he spake unto his people saying 'Help me with your strength until I have placed a wall between you and them' . . . . Thus he shut in Gog and Magog and the nations that were akin to them . . . . And he sealed with a double seal the gate between the divine children of Adam and Gog and Magog, who also are the children of Adam, but who are like beasts." There, in the Outer Darkness, the filthy people will remain enclosed behind high walls and a metal gate whence they will emerge with the advent of the Antichrist. "When the thousands years are expired," prophesizes Saint John, "Satan shall be loosed out of his prison, And shall go out to deceive the nations which are in the four corners of the earth, Gog and Magog, to gather them together to battle: the number of whom is as the sands of the sea."

The Barbarians, as we have already noted, are numerous. They lurk around the small enclave the Civilized Man had conquered for himself. They are either enclosed, as are temporarily the people of Gog and Magog, or they live on the edges of the world, in the "four corners," i.e., in lands in which the circular dome of the sky does not cover the earth that is square.

The Foreigner, the Stranger, may be "strange," even grotesque, but his deformity is funny rather than horrible. Why should we be afraid of the Sciapodes, men who covered themselves with the shadow of their only foot? We are amused rather than frightened by men whose feet are turned backward and who have eight toes on each foot, by men with ears so large that they use them as cloaks, by dwarfs who have no mouth but only a round hole through which they suck their

260
A hermaphrodite

261
A man with a long neck and a sharp beak

262

A Cannibal

Engraving from Dati's Secondo Cantare, *Rome, 1494-95*
Lilly Rare Book Library, Indiana University

Cannibals, living somewhere in India, are described by the translator of Columbus' Letter (announcing his discovery) as rich and powerful and totally naked save for elaborate gold earrings.

263

Saint Christopher as a horse-faced knight

From an unidentified Russian manuscript

264

Dog-faced Men as Cannibals

Engraving from Fries' Underweisung und uszlegung Der Cartha Marina . . ., *Strasbourg, 1530*
Lilly Rare Book Library, Indiana University

food with the aid of a tube? We hear of people without necks. In a certain land all people have a hole in the middle of their chest; the notables of that country are carried by means of a pole that passes through this hole. What is surprising in surveying these oddities is not the richness, but the poverty of human imagination. The variations in the descriptions of these strange peoples are only slight; the same descriptions crop up again and again, from Greece to Western Europe, from the Middle East to China.

The Barbarian may be human but only barely so; his abodes are outside the human *oikoumene*. He lives in the Outer Darkness, in the North, the place where the sun does not shine for months on end, whence blows the deadly north wind. The Barbarian, pressing on the borders of the civilized world already tinted by its influence, is but the vanguard of the menacing monsters behind him, perhaps behind the Wall, who constitute the real menace to humanity. The Foreigner is only strange or grotesque; they are outright monstrous, with a monstrosity which is not accidental but functional, revealing their real identity.

Perhaps the Monster is horse-hoofed, as is the Devil of the Western world. The *Hippopodes,* a people born with horses' feet, were known to Greeks, Romans, and Chinese. Both the Greeks and the Chinese reported the existence of dog-headed monsters who, they thought, might have inhabited a part of India or the deserts along the coast of the Ocean that surrounds the earth. Attila the Hun was frequently portrayed with a dog's head. Dog-headed men are represented on many romanesque churches in France, symbolizing the ultimate triumph of Christ, to whom even the Monsters do homage. In a little known variant of the Saint Christopher legend, the giant saint ferrying Christ across the river is just a poor Barbarian called the Reprobate— he is dog-headed.

The role of the Monsters is essential. Thanks to them, we, the Civilized, learn to appreciate the advantages of the society we live in. "Order" exists only in relation to "disorder." The joys of wealth can be appreciated only by contrasting them with the plights of poverty. But is there no cement stronger than self-righteousness to hold a society together? Apparently no human society can survive without outside pressure. Again and again people who make up a human group seem to lose faith in the criteria that define their congregation. Only the spectre that looms beyond the border prevents disintegration.

Fortunately for all of us, the Barbarian, the Monster, has a unique quality: if he does not exist, he can always be conjured up. Obediently, he will appear, strange, monstrous, bearing upon himself the marks of an existence made miserable by his separateness from our own community. His appearance alone suffices to recreate a feeling of solidarity. We may have our own troubles—sickness, poverty, war, hunger—but at least we have human heads, and limbs, and civilized manners. *Tout est pour le mieux dans le meilleur des mondes.*

265

The Wall Built by Alexander the Great to Contain Gog and Magog

Miniature from the Matali al-Sa'ada wa-manabi al-sidaya, *or "Treatises on Astrology and Divination," Turkish, 1582*
The Pierpont Morgan Library

The notion that wild tribes of men, who must be held back lest they overrun the world, existed on the outer fringes of Asia is echoed in the Bible and in the Koran. This intricate and confusing legend became attached to the Oriental version of Alexander's story. Alexander, now called Iskander and also Dulcarnain, the Two-Horned One, is charged by the Almighty with building a great wall and imprisoning within its gates the peoples called Gog and Magog. The location of this concentration camp is variously situated all the way from Derbend in the Caucasus to the far reaches of Northeastern Mongolia. The names Gog and Magog have been interpreted as referring to the Goths and Mogols, and also to the Lost Tribes of Israel, and sometimes to two giants acting as guardians of the Gates.

In the Turkish miniature illustrated here, the artist shows a few hapless people trying to stay out of the way of a devouring serpent. At the top of the wall are posted two horsemen, a trumpeter, and a drummer, whose duty is to make a constant din so that the captives will believe that Alexander's army is on the watch. A related legend says that in time the sound of the drum and trumpet was muffled by the feathers shed by owls. The Mongols finally escaped and overran Europe, and ever since have worn owls' feathers in their hats out of gratitude.

265

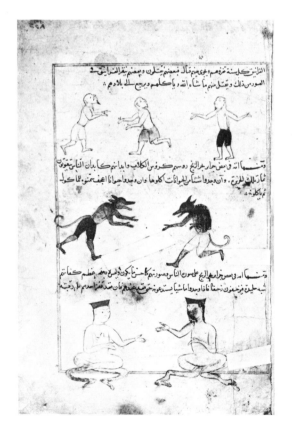

266

The Guildhall Giants, Gog and Magog, by Richard Saunders

Guildhall, London, 1708 (wood)

These fourteen-foot figures used to stand in niches outside the Guildhall, but were brought inside during the war and have remained there. There are conflicting stories about them. One is that they are descendents of the Emperor Diocletian, and another is they are figurations of the Antichrist, and, as such, remotely related to the Scythians, Tatars, and other scourges of mankind. Since the time of Henry V, they have discharged the menial functions of porters of the royal palaces.

267

Various Races of Men Contained Within Alexander's Wall

Illustrations from a Persian version of Kazwini's Cosmography, *16th century*
New York Public Library, Spencer Collection

Dog-headed men can be recognized in the middle group.

268

A Chinese version of headless being shown in figure 258 above

Here he is regarded as a heavenly spirit.

Extraordinary Creatures Living Beyond the Celestial Kingdom

Illustrations from a modern printing of the "Hills and Streams Classic" (China, ca. 3d century B.C.) Cambridge University Library

269

The dog-bodied monster who lives in the region to the east of China

270

People with holes in their chests

271

Extraordinary Creatures and Customs
Illustrations from Hokusai's Manga
Indiana University Fine Arts Library

A double page from Manga XII (1834) showing "Moxa-burning in foreign lands"

The Japanese believed that this popular cure, which consists of applying burning pellets of punk to an afflicted part of the body in order to stimulate nerve-ends, was universally practiced.

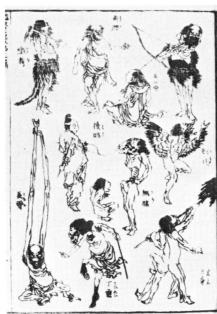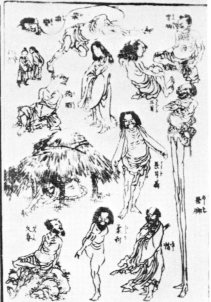

272

A double page from Manga III (1815)

Dog-headed men, men with long ears, pygmies, and other monsters familiar in Western mythology will be recognized here.

273

A Japanese Knight, by H. von Wiering

German, 1685 (woodcut)
Library of Congress

In contrast to figure 274, here is a Japanese warrior as imagined by a seventeenth-century German artist. Save for the two samurai swords, every aspect of the subject is based on preconceived notions having little to do with reality.

Of all countries in the world Japan was the most consistently and effectively closed to visitors from the outside—an exclusion which affected even the Chinese at various epochs. Europeans were permitted to land about the end of the sixteenth century, but they were normally restricted to the port of Nagasaki. This accounts for the rise of a school of art known as *Nagasaki-E,* best known for its portrayal of Westerners. Many of these representations have a satirical bite which the West does not fail to appreciate.

The Portuguese warrior portrayed here looks outlandish in the fullest sense of the word. He wears a kimono and his hair is done in Japanese style, but the ruff and the full-bottomed trousers are European. The Soldier of Christ, the Man of Peace, holds a crucifix in one hand and an arquebus in the other; the symbolism may not have escaped the Japanese.

274

A Portuguese Warrior

Panel from a Namban or "Foreigner" Screen, ca. 1600 (color and gold leaf on paper) Seattle Art Museum, Mrs. Thomas D. Stimson Memorial

Picture of a Busy America, attributed to
Hiroshige III

Japanese, ca. 1860 (woodblock print as a triptych)
The Art Institute of Chicago, Emily Crane Chad-
bourne Collection

The Japanese curiosity about America which followed immediately after Commodore Perry's landing entailed a certain amount of confusion. The
scene depicted here is actually the square before
Friedricksborg Castle in Copenhagen.

275

276
An American Lady
Nagasaki, ca. 1875 (woodblock print)
Library of Congress

This view of an Amazon wearing an Indian feather
headdress and riding a mustang was obviously inspired by an early Japanese version of a Wild West
story.

277
Commodore Perry
Nagasaki, after 1856
Library of Congress
(woodblock print)

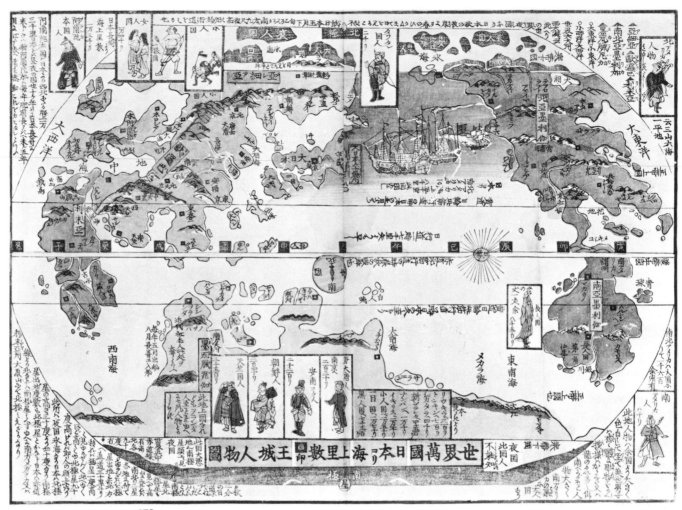

278

Japanese Map of the World

Early 19th century (woodblock print as a diptych)
Library of Congress

At this late date odd creatures such as one-eyed men, pygmies, giants, and Amazons are shown sharing the world with the Chinese, and the South Americans.

279

English Handbill

Ca. 1855

Library of Congress

Chinese people as well as Chinese objects of art and curios were articles of export in the second half of the nineteenth century, the former mainly as objects of display. Curiosity about the "appearance, manners and peculiarities of the people of the Central Flowery Kingdom" was fed by faithful reconstitution of the Chinese habitat and the presence of natives capable of "affording much information to Visitors."

RECEPTION OF THE CHINESE FAMILY BY HER MAJESTY, AT OSBORNE.

280
Reception of the Chinese Family by Her Majesty, at Osborne
English, about 1855 (engraving)
Library of Congress

281
European Curios on View in Peking, by Honoré Daumier
French, about 1859 (lithograph)
Library of Congress

282
Mounted Archer
From Suessula, Campania, early 5th century B.C.
(bronze)
Norbert Schimmel Collection, Kings Point, New
York

The Mysterious Scythians

284
Horse and Rider
Chinese, T'ang dynasty or earlier
(tomb figurine, pottery)
The Metropolitan Museum of Art, Gift of C. T. Loo,
1916

283
Scythians Pledging Brotherhood by Drinking
Blood
Siberia, ca. 5th or 4th century B.C. (bronze plaque)
The Hermitage, Leningrad

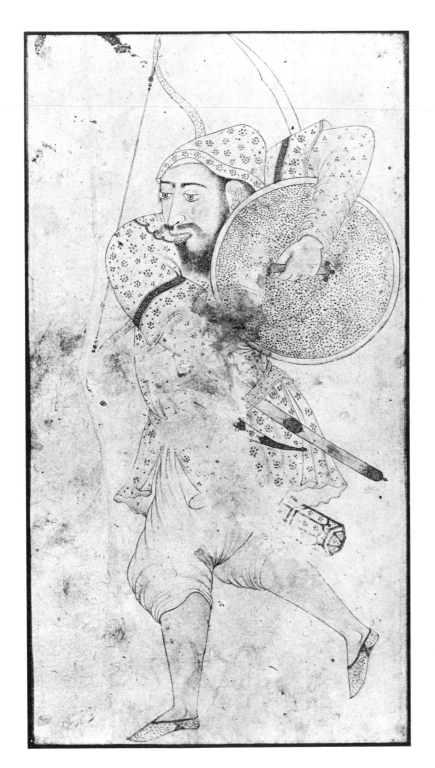

285
Mongolian Warrior
Persian, ca. 1400 (miniature)
Museum of Fine Arts, Boston

There is a strong likelihood that this is an accurate portrayal of a foot soldier in one of Tamerlane's armies.

286
A Tartar Monarch, by H. von Wiering
German, ca. 1685 (wood engraving)
Library of Congress

This "Tartar-Chan" wears a costume not unlike that
worn by Hungarians and Turks in the seventeenth
century.

Persi- aner.

287
A Persian Guard and Lady, by H. von Wiering
German, ca. 1685 (wood engraving)
Library of Congress

In 1721 Montesquieu made fun, in his *Persian Letters*, of the immense popularity which Persian visitors enjoyed in Paris. That this was entirely due to their outlandish dress is proved by the fact that when they changed into French clothing nobody paid them the slightest attention. When a Persian gentleman, not wearing his native dress, was introduced into polite society, all he got by way of response was: *"Monsieur est persan? Comment peut-on être persan?"*

FOR FURTHER READING

A. R. Anderson, *Alexander's Gate, Gog and Magog, and the Inclosed Nations,* 1932.

J. Baltrusaïtis, *Le Moyen Age Fantastique,* 1955.

R. Wittkower, "Marvels of the East; a Study in the History of Monsters," *Journal of the Warburg Institute,* V (1942), pp. 159-196.

IX

THEODORE BOWIE:

Iconography of the Universal Hero

THE THEME OF THE UNIVERSAL HERO SUBSUMES THOSE OTHER ASPECTS OF THE EAST-WEST INFLUENCE IN ART— AWARENESS, DIFFUSION, AND MUTUAL INTERACTION—SINCE the common subject implies social and political unity between the two parts of the world. While universality would seem to be a natural feature of religion, no religious figure—Christ, Mohammed, or Buddha —could embody the myth suitably. Islam came close to being a world religion when it reached in one direction across the Mediterranean as far as Spain, and in the other, through India and Southeast Asia as far as the Philippines, and it is still a mighty force in many parts of this immense territory. Yet no Islamic leader came to be regarded as a world hero. Islam lacked central authority and political unity. Revered in the East and admired in the West during the Middle Ages and in the Romantic period, Saladin was almost the only Mohammedan **290** figure to have fired imaginations over the world but he was scarcely a universal hero.

The only candidates for this grand role have been autocratic and martial personages driven to conquer the world or large portions thereof. Asian conquerors such as Attila, Genghiz Khan and Kublai **288** Khan, and Tamerlane in their time ruled great stretches of the Eurasian continent, but are likely to be looked upon as destroyers rather than as unifiers of the world. The works of art that confer immortality upon historic personages in this group are few indeed. Attila's repute is wretched; Voltaire made of Genghiz Khan a European father-figure in **289** his play *L'Orphelin de la Chine*. Kublai Khan, thanks to Coleridge, is a household word for us, but not much else. Tamerlane's imposing reputation in Western literature rests primarily on Marlowe's *Tamburlaine the Great,* though it has only rarely been produced in the nearly 400 years of its existence.

Tamerlane (1336?-1405) was not a Mongol but a Turk, although he **292** claimed to be a descendant of Genghiz Khan, and his empire during his lifetime never included China. Two visitors from the West—one, an Arab, and the other Spanish—who were sent on missions to him, have left the only first-hand descriptions, altogether too brief, of this tremendous figure. The celebrated Tunisian historian, Ibn Khaldun, visited Tamerlane in 1401 while the latter was besieging Damascus. He was well received, and Tamerlane asked the visitor searching questions about his country of origin (the Maghrib). About the only personal detail noted by Ibn Khaldun was his physical limitation: owing to the knee injury which earned him the nickname, "The Lame," Tamerlane had to be carried by his men and lifted onto his horse. Two years later, Don Ruy Gonzalez de Clavijo, ambassador of the King of Spain, reached Tamerlane's court at Samarkand. He describes Tamerlane only as "so old that his eyelids had fallen down entirely," and we are given no glimpse of the personality or character of the ruler who so lavishly entertained his Spanish guest.

The process of mythmaking seems better served by the absense of first-hand documentation than by its existence, a truth further demonstrated by the legend of Prester John. This figure who may be the fig- **291** ment of many imaginations is the lone Christian candidate for the post

288
Attila

From Paolo Giovio, Elogia Virorum Bellica Virtute
Illustrium, *Basel, 1575*
Yale University Library

289

Chinghiz Khan Crowned King of the Tartars

Illumination in Le Livre des Merveilles de l'Asie
The Pierpont Morgan Library

Marco Polo tells us that Genghiz Khan (1167-1227) was elected the First Khan of the Tartars in the year 1187. He describes him as *"homs de grant valeur, de grant sens et de grant prouesse,"* capable of earning the devotion of innumerable followers who helped him conquer a large portion of the globe. There are no reliable portraits of him.

290
Saladin

From Paolo Giovio, Elogia Virorum Bellica . . .
Yale University Library

Abu'l-Muzaffar Yusuf ibn Ayyub, also called Salah al-Din or Saladin (1137-1193) was as highly regarded in his time by his subjects as by the Franks whom he fought and who helped to immortalize him along with his great adversary, Richard, Coeur-de-Lion. He appears in Tasso's *Jerusalem Delivered* as well as in Scott's *The Talisman.*

291

Prester John of the Indies

Woodcut illustration from Dati, Secondo Cantare,
Rome, 1493
The British Museum, London

292

Tamerlan, Empereur des Tartares

From Thevet, Les Vrais Pourtraits des Hommes Il-
lustres, *Paris, 1584*
Yale University Library

293
Timour-lenk
Engraving in Witsen, Noord en Oost Tartaryen, v. I,
Amsterdam, 1705
Lilly Rare Book Library, Indiana University

294
Tamerlane
From the Nuremberg Chronicle, *1493*
Lilly Rare Book Library, Indiana University

of world ruler, a kind of Pope whose see shifted from Mongolia to Ethiopia. Marco Polo firmly believed in his existence, and reported that Genghiz Khan had defeated him in battle and had absorbed his realm. In 1165 the Pope in Rome, the Emperor of Byzantium, and various other Western rulers received a *Letter* from this priest-king in which he announced his intention of helping to liberate the Holy Land from the Infidels. The existence of such a fabulous Christian theocratic ally in Asia continued to be taken seriously for centuries thereafter. In the sixteenth century Prester John's realm was definitely located in Ethiopia, and there is report of·a mission by the Portuguese monk Francisco Alvarez to his court.

Alexander the Great has had a far greater influence on art and literature than any of these Eastern leaders. The Macedonian conqueror is scarcely the most virtuous or magnanimous figure. Yet he fulfills most requirements of the universal hero: aesthetic appeal, personal courage, political sagicity, intellectual curiosity, historical importance, and the quality of being all things to all men in the East as well as the West. He consciously willed the political unity of the immense territory he was invading; only a fluke prevented him from conquering all of India and China. This disciple of Aristotle who acquired an Eastern mentality kindled romantic enthusiasm in widely distant places over many centuries in a great variety of ways. In his lifetime he destroyed the Achaemenian Empire and caused the dispersal of Persian craftsmen; at the same time he caused great Asian cities to be built. As a figure in history he inspired countless artists, poets, playwrights, novelists, philosophers, historians, and archaeologists. Finally the man became a legend and his life a myth in at least three guises: Alexander, the Western conqueror and adventurer; Iskander, the Eastern sage and explorer; and Dulcarnain, the protector of Islam. *(Cont. on page 189)*

295

Timur Before a Battle

From the Manuscript of the Zafar Namah *or History of Timur, by Sharaf ad Din Ali Yazdi: Persian, Timurid School, ca. 1450 (miniature)*
The Metropolitan Museum of Art, Purchase, 1955, Rogers Fund

This miniature was painted, probably in Shiraz, some fifty years after Tamerlane's death; the portrait may hence be regarded as fairly reliable.

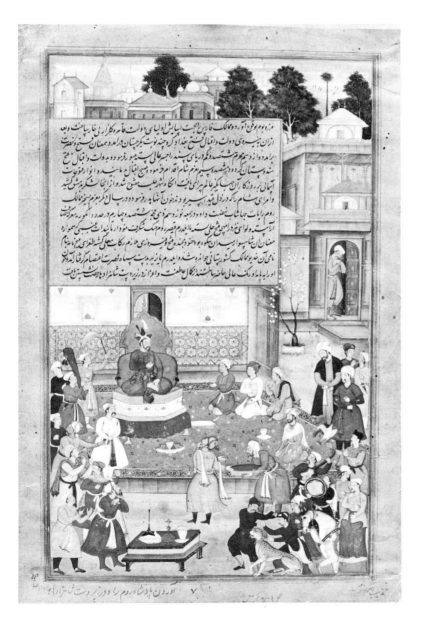

296

The Emperor Timur Receiving Turkish Princes
Who Have Been Taken Prisoner

From the Timur Namah (*or* History of the House of
Timur) *by Dharam Das: Persian, ca. 1600 (miniature)*
The Metropolitan Museum of Art, Purchase, 1935,
Rogers Fund

Like his European contemporaries, the Mughal artist is heedless of historical versimilitude, and por-
trays Tamerlane and Alexander in the same fashion
that he would limn any descendant of Akbar.

297

Map of the World

From Ortelius, Theatrum Orbis Terrarum, *Antwerp, 1570*

Lilly Rare Book Library, Indiana University

Marlowe was familiar with this great Atlas. It can be assumed that this is the map which is brought to the dying Tamerlane in Act V, scene 3, of the second part of *Tamburlaine the Great,* when he reviews his lifetime of conquests before his sons:

Give me a map; then let me see how much
Is left for me to conquer all the world,
That these, my boys, may finish all my wants.
Here I began to march towards Persia,
Along Armenia and the Caspian Sea,
And then unto Bithynia, where I took
The Turk and his great empress prisoners.
There I marched into Egypt and Arabia;
And here, not far from Alexandria,
Where the Terrene and the Red Sea meet,
Being distant less than full a hundred leagues,
I meant to cut a channel to them both,
That men might quickly sail to India.
From thence to Nubia near Borno lake,
And so along the Ethiopian sea,
Cutting the tropic line of Capricorn,
I conquered all as far as Zanzibar.
Then by the northern part of Africa,
I came at last to Graecia, and from thence
To Asia, where I stay against my will;
Which is from Scythia, where I first began,
Backwards and forwards near five thousand
   leagues.
Look here, my boys, see what a world of ground
Lies westward from the midst of Cancer's line
Unto the rising of this earthly globe.
Whereas the sun, declining from our sight,
Begins the day with our Antipodes!
And shall I die, and this unconquered?
Lo, here, my sons, are the golden mines,
Inestimable and precious stones,
More worth than Asia and the world beside;
And from th'Antarctic Pole eastward behold
As much more land which never was descried,
Wherein are rocks of pearl that shine as bright
As all the lamps that beautify the sky!
And shall I die, and this unconquered?

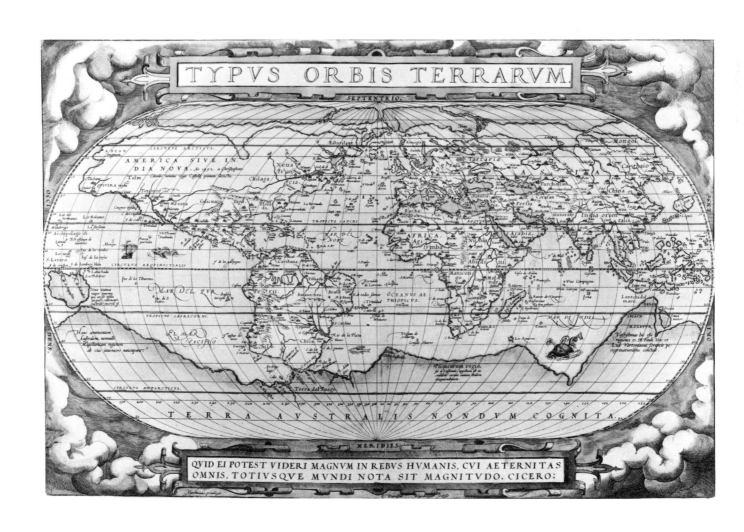

TYPVS ORBIS TERRARVM

QVID EI POTEST VIDERI MAGNVM IN REBVS HVMANIS, CVI AETERNITAS
OMNIS, TOTIVSQVE MVNDI NOTA SIT MAGNITVDO. CICERO:

298
Head of Alexander as Herakles

Hellenistic, 3d century (?) (bronze applique:
ht., 4 in.)
Burton H. Berry Loan Collection, Indiana University

299
Alexander the Great

Found in Egypt, dated 2nd century B.C. (alabaster
bust: ht., 9 in.)
The Brooklyn Museum

300
Alexander the Great Hunting
Coptic, 8th or 9th century (embroidered roundel, wool)
The Textile Museum Collection, Washington, D.C.

The hero, shown on horseback in reverse image and holding the torch symbolizing the life of the intellect, is being crowned by a pair of angels.

301
Head of Alexander with Horns
Macedonian, 3d century B.C. (silver coin)
Burton H. Berry Loan Collection, Indiana University

302
Ascension of Alexander
Possibly Anatolian, 12th century (bronze mirror: diam. 2⅜ in.)
University of Michigan Art Museum Collection, Ann Arbor

303
Alexander the Great

From Paolo Giovio, Elogium Virorum Bellica . . .
Yale University Library

304
Alexander as a Medieval Knight

Colored woodcut from the Nuremberg Chronicle
Lilly Rare Book Library, Indiana University

305

**Triumphal Entry of Alexander into Babylon,
by S. Leclerc**

French, ca. 1650 (engraving)
The Metropolitan Museum of Art

This engraving reproduces the enormous canvas by
Charles Le Brun, which is now in the Louvre. The
cartouche reads, "Thus through Virtue do Heroes
reach the heights."

306

Darius III, by J. Sadeler

German, 17th century (engraving)
The Metropolitan Museum of Art

The last of the Achaemenian kings is regarded by
modern historians as a wise ruler and administrator.
After his death from wounds received in battle, he
was given an honorable burial by Alexander, who
treated his widow and children with utmost mag-
nanimity. In the Eastern version of the Alexander
legend, Iskander is considered to be a younger
brother to Darius and therefore his legitimate successor.

307
Alexander Fights a Sea-battle in China
*Illumination from a Mughal version of Nizami's poem by Dharam Das, about 1595
The Metropolitan Museum of Art, Gift of Alexander Smith Cochran, 1913*

308 Alexander and the Seven Sages

Miniature from a version of Nizami's Khamsah executed in Herat during the second half of the 15th century
The Metropolitan Museum of Art, Gift of Alexander Smith Cochran, 1913

The seven sages are Plato, Aristotle, Hippocrates, Thales, Hermes Trismegistus, Apollonius, and Porphyry. Each philosopher is giving his account of Creation.
Nizami's poem falls into two parts: *Sikander Nama e Bara*, in which the hero is treated as Conqueror of the World; and *Sikander Nama e Bahri,* in which he appears as Philosopher and Prophet, as well as Traveler.

309

Alexander Receiving Advice from Plato

From the Mughal version of the Khamsah, by Dharam Das, about 1595
The Metropolitan Museum of Art, Gift of Alexander Smith Cochran, 1913

310

The Gymnosophists

Engraving from Theodore de Bry, India Orientalis, Frankfort, 1613
Lilly Rare Book Library, Indiana University

Plutarch recounts the meeting of Alexander with the eight Yogis or Brahmins to whom he puts a number of questions: "Which are the most numerous, the living or the dead?", "Which is the craftiest of all animals?", "Which is older, the day or the night?" He was so pleased by their answers that he sent them away loaded with presents, though their philosophy prescribed the renunciation of all worldly goods.

188 / *East-West in Art*

The legendary figure alone appears in more than ninety versions, extending from Iceland to Mongolia, in a number of languages which include Greek, Latin, Syriac, Amharic, Arabic, French, English, Spanish, Italian, German, Moldavian, Russian, Persian, Hindi, Burmese, and Malayan. Only Chinese and Japanese are conspicuously absent. Japan rigorously held out against foreign importations of all kinds more consistently than any other Asian country, although Alexander's personality would have superbly suited the great epic tradition in that country. The Chinese during the Han period were certainly aware of a great conqueror, whom they called Lek Yan. In the period from Alexander's death to the sixteenth century, his legend passed back and forth endlessly between East and West. Through these mutual borrowings Alexander became the ideal hero in both parts of the world.

When other forms replaced epic poetry as the primary literary expression, Alexander became the subject of innumerable tragedies, operas, and ballets, among them, Racine's *Alexandre,* Lyly's *Alexander and Campaspe,* and Lee's *Alexander the Great or the Rival Queens.* Metastasio's play on this subject furnished material for more than fifty operas by such renowned composers as Glück, Paisiello, Cimarosa, and Cherubini. Alexander's real and imaginary adventures also motivated the invention of such literary *genres* as science fiction and the relation of fabulous journeys.

The depiction of Christ as *Pantocrator* on Byzantine churches has been linked to Alexander's role as conqueror and ruler of the world. Between the end of the Renaissance and the early nineteenth century, he was the subject of some notable canvasses by Raphael, Sodoma, Altdorfer, Jan Brueghel, Le Brun, and Delacroix. The theme of the universal hero has little relevance for the present-day artist; now it is the historian and archaeologist who are inspired by Alexander.

FOR FURTHER READING

A. Abel, *Le Roman d'Alexandre,* 1928.

H. W. Clarke, *The Sikander Nama e Bara,* 1881.

M. Bieber, *Alexander the Great in Greek and Roman Art,* 1964.

R. Grousset, *Conquérant du Monde,* 1944.

————, *L'Empire des Steppes,* 1960.

C. Mercer, *Alexander the Great,* 1962.

V. Slessarev, *Prester John, the Letter and the Legend,* 1959.

M. A. Stein, *On Alexander's Track to the Indus,* 1929.

W. W. Tarn, *The Greeks in Bactria and India,* 1951.